The Disfiguration of Nature

The Disfiguration of Nature

Why Caring for the Environment is Inherently Conservative

JAMES G. KRUEGER

Foreword by Eric T. Freyfogle

WIPF & STOCK · Eugene, Oregon

THE DISFIGURATION OF NATURE
Why Caring for the Environment is Inherently Conservative

Copyright © 2018 James G. Krueger. All rights reserved. Except for brief quotations in critical publications or reviews, no part of this book may be reproduced in any manner without prior written permission from the publisher. Write: Permissions, Wipf and Stock Publishers, 199 W. 8th Ave., Suite 3, Eugene, OR 97401.

Wipf & Stock
An Imprint of Wipf and Stock Publishers
199 W. 8th Ave., Suite 3
Eugene, OR 97401

www.wipfandstock.com

PAPERBACK ISBN: 978-1-5326-5480-0
HARDCOVER ISBN: 978-1-5326-5481-7
EBOOK ISBN: 978-1-5326-5482-4

Manufactured in the U.S.A.   10/17/18

All Wendell Berry quotes copyright © 1977 by Wendell Berry. Reprinted by permission of Counterpoint Press.

Unless otherwise indicated, all Bible verses are quoted from the Revised Standard Version Second Catholic Edition.

For Maureen and for these mountains,
who never cease to put me in my place.

Our age could be characterized as a manifold experiment in faithlessness, and if it has as yet produced no effective understanding of the practicalities of faith, it has certainly produced massive evidence of the damage and disorder of its absence.[1]

—Wendell Berry, *The Unsettling of America*

For no thing can there be any completeness that is outside its own nature, and no thing for which there is any advance save in its own kind. If this were not so, all nature by now would have dissolved in chaos and folly, nothing in it, neither its own self nor any other.[2]

—Stark Young, "I'll Take My Stand"

---

1. Berry, *Unsettling of America*, 125.
2. Young, "Not in Memoriam," 359.

Contents

Foreword by Eric T. Freyfogle — ix
Preface — xv
Acknowledgements — xix

Introduction — 1

Chapter 1
Conservation: A Brief History — 16

Chapter 2
Wrongheaded About Rights — 36

Chapter 3
Husbandmen, Households, and Economies — 55

Chapter 4
Abortion and the Earth — 69

Chapter 5
LGBTQ Narratives and the Love of Nature — 85

Chapter 6
Technological Infatuations and Membership with the Land — 114

Chapter 7
Coming Home — 132

Bibliography — 147

Foreword

ERIC T. FREYFOGLE

I BEGAN JAMES KRUEGER's book anticipating I would dislike it and quietly hoping, I suspect and now confess, I'd find quick cause to set it aside. It didn't happen. I begin with this point because I'm confident other readers will crack his covers with the same prejudgment and, blinders in place, will underestimate the work and miss its extraordinary content. As the title and subtitle suggest, the book has to do with political thought, and with the natural world and our place in it. It has much to say about environmentalism and about the movement's current spot on the political spectrum. But the book journeys more widely than these topics suggest, along the way drawing surprising and revealing connections, probing to unusual depths, and ultimately—I suspect—leaving most readers disoriented.

What a respectful reader soon perceives is that Krueger is an original and forceful moralist. Of course he laments our divided politics, but he does so only in passing, anxious to get on to his bigger tasks, to his observations on the whole community of life, and to his bracing precepts on the kind of culture we'll need to foster healing and wholeness, in ourselves and our surrounding biotic wholes. Krueger cares deeply about nature and about people. He yearns for us all, linked together, to head in a better direction, and soon. Though he organizes his points logically and calmly, his work is nonetheless best taken as a cry from the heart, as the outpouring of a soul saddened by ill health in our natural world, by declines in public and private morality, and by the superficial, miscast, histrionic politics that keep us from grasping our existential plight and making overdue, sharp corrections to our trajectories—intellectual, moral, and political. Few readers will agree with all that Krueger has to say; I for one did not. But no reader will doubt his sincerity, nor will any fair reader find even his harshest stances easy to dismiss.

Krueger's manuscript arrived on my desk at a timely moment. A national conservation organization on whose board of directors I serve had just completed a new strategic plan. The plan called for heightened attention to the cultural causes and contexts of our misuses of nature; for the crafting, it stated rather simplistically, of a "new conservation ethic." The subject was one I had engaged for years, and I was vocal in promoting the plank. Environmental groups can clearly see what we humans are doing wrong in nature. They do less well getting to the *why* issue, to the true root causes of our bad behavior, many of them cultural. How can we foster real change in our abusive behaviors if we don't lay bare and transform the cultural components that cause our current behaviors to seem appropriate, if not inevitable?

As I expected, the national group now struggles with this challenge (indeed, struggles to even comprehend the issue, given the larger movement's tendency to dwell on facts, economics, and politics). They want all people to respect nature—to love it, even—and they know about nature's ecological interconnections. But at the same time, they embrace individual human rights, particularly liberty and equality, and they are as prone as their neighbors to comprehend humans chiefly as autonomous individuals, free to set their own courses and liberated from dated, constraining traditions. What they experience and display in their struggles is the awkwardness of being at once a modern, open-minded, free-roaming social liberal and an advocate for the disciplined, responsible use of nature's incredible richness. The way to bridge the gap they sense (as do their counterparts in other groups) is to promote the love of nature as an individual choice—the best choice, of course—and to encourage individuals everywhere to craft and embrace a personal land ethic.

What too few environmentalists see is that the presumptions of modern liberal individualism, all across the political spectrum, collide with a view of nature as interconnected and interdependent. Similarly, to deem nature worthy of respect—to treat the care of nature as a moral imperative—is to presume that we humans are duty-bound to tailor our ways of living so as to acknowledge a larger moral order beyond our choosing. So, is morality simply a matter of respecting the individual rights of others, or might we live and breathe in a natural order that imposes other, stronger demands? Krueger is not the first to expose these tensions, but few have

Foreword

done this so lucidly. At bottom, a humble, ecologically informed view of the natural world, one that acknowledges the limits on human knowledge and power, one which clashes sharply with many now-dominant views about the independence and the moral freedom of the individual human. More broadly, a nature-respecting environmentalism is not, at its foundation, a liberal school of thought. To embrace liberalism in the human social realm, while putting out the call to respect nature, is to create intellectual and moral tensions that inevitably sow confusion.

As well as anyone Krueger has succeeded in getting to the bottom of our disjunction with nature. Even better, he has advice to offer on the kind of culture we need if we are to live in ways that sustain health and productivity in our world. That reformed culture, he explains, overlaps considerably with what he terms true conservatism, or what others might call paleo-conservatism. This is not the laissez-faire, market-worshipping, government-hating polemical view of most of today's self-styled conservatives. These are, Krueger tells us, just a particular manifestation of liberalism, one that accentuates economic liberty and gun rights rather than rights to an abortion or gay marriage. He has in mind instead a much older, more respectful conservatism, one that holds high relationships, integrity, humility, and responsibility. Krueger calls this an older conservatism, and in some ways it is. Yet Krueger has stood ready to cut and prune older ideas and to graft new ones to the point where his conservatism offers a distinct freshness that separates it from the world of, say, Edmund Burke and Thomas Carlyle (and, more recently, Richard Weaver). When Krueger says in his subtitle that care of the environment is a conservative cause, one needs to go slow. He means it is not inherently liberal, and he is right. Beyond that, the reader is advised to set aside presumptions and to listen and learn.

Krueger clearly wants the environmental cause to succeed. It is from this stance that he calls sharply for the movement to cut its apparent ties with other causes that, in fact, are left-liberal. Environmental policies, he contends, would gain greater support if voters did not, when voting green, also have to vote (for instance) pro-choice and pro-LGBTQ rights. Many old-style conservatives in Krueger's view are inclined to vote for the responsible use of nature, but are diverted from doing so because the politicians who promote strong protective measures also endorse unrelated, left-liberal policies that they reject. The left-liberal stance of the environmental cause, that is, does more than breed confusion and keep environmental advocates from clearly seeing the true moral grounds for responsible land use. It costs votes, saps political strength, and leads to missed chances to improve the ways we dwell in nature. The environmental cause, he recommends, should somehow shove itself off, cutting ties as openly as it can with these controversial, left-liberal causes, the pro-choice cause above all.

Many readers who travel with Krueger to this point might well ask: whose fault is this current arrangement, and what, realistically, is the environmental cause supposed to do about it? Green groups openly seek votes from any politician willing to support them. Can one fault them if their political supporters these days also support causes that, as Krueger highlights, build on a different moral foundation? If they cut ties with their current political friends, who is to help them? Yes, they logically belong with and among voters who embrace the kind of old-style conservatism that Krueger promotes, a conservatism that honors communities, multiple-generations, relationships, integrity, and binding duties. But there aren't many such voters, as Krueger himself laments, and so where are they to head?

It is at this point that one suspects Krueger has a more ambitious aim than simply pulling the environmental cause rightward and encouraging more conservatives to support it. He has little good to say about today's right-side, pro-market libertarians, masquerading as conservative, so he's not encouraging environmentalists to join ranks with them. What he likely wants, in truth, is for a new conservative force to arise in our society, one that displaces liberals on both the far right and the far left. And he not only wants the environmental movement to be part of this new conservative force, but he wants the movement to help bring it about, to be a central, formative element of it. It is an intriguing—if not compelling—cultural and moral vision. What if, in fact, our culture did shift so that we phrased our competing ideas not, as now, in terms of clashing individual rights, but instead in terms of how well our respective ideas promote the common good and sustain the health, productivity, and beauty of our landscapes, farms, towns, and cities? What if we accentuated, not our autonomy and freedom of choice, but the many ways that the links between and among us not only sustain our health but go far in defining who we are? What if we yearned collectively for ways to live with greater integrity, honing and elevating the elements of good citizenship?

In Krueger's view, a new moral order of the type he promotes will be one that returns many people to the land, living and working on family-sized farms that are diverse enough to provide direct sustenance for the

FOREWORD

people living there. He acknowledges, though likely not clearly enough for some readers, the challenges of making this vision a reality, not the least because current farm policies, set by agri-business, so effectively stifle small farms economically. Like other promoters of a pastoral vision, Krueger also seems quick to assume the environmental virtue of small farms; historically and even today, their environmental records are quite mixed. Then there are the longstanding social dynamics of agrarian household life, with its long history of especially harsh burdens and limits on women. Krueger scoffs at those today (environmental groups among them) who seek to help economically depressed rural areas by pushing eco-tourism and green jobs, including solar and wind farms. He is right—local people might wish that other forms of good-paying work came along instead. But massive changes in laws and public policies are needed for that to happen, changes of a type that environmental groups could never bring about.

For many readers, the hardest parts of Krueger's book will be those in which he engages the issues of abortion and LGBTQ rights. Here readers need to tread with particular care if they are to see why these topics enter the book at all and why Krueger seems to go out of his way, when challenging pro-choice, and pro-LGBTQ stances, to present and attack them in their most extreme rhetorical forms. Krueger wants to root out cultural values that are leading us astray, and one sees them most starkly in their more extreme forms. On his side, Krueger's rhetoric is also deliberately bracing, intended to put the reader on the defensive. Some at this point may toss the book aside. Those who don't will find themselves arguing with Krueger in a dialectic that just might bear fruit. Some will say Krueger overlooks the issue of overpopulation (as he does) and the natural inclinations among many species, and many early people, to practice infanticide. On the LGBTQ issue, as well, he skims over the groundings of homosexuality in nature and the ways evolutionary pressures might sensibly keep homosexual genes in circulation. As a population control measure, is abortion worse than war or starvation? Then, too, there are countless people who find abortion morally troubling but who balk at legal bans, knowing how they affect poor women most of all, while leaving wealthier ones free to get abortions in places where legal or to employ today's cheap, abortion-inducing drugs. On abortion, the legal and moral issues are far from identical. But to admit this is not really to counter Krueger's cultural claims. At a deeper level, he is on to something about the inconsistency of respecting nature in some settings and ignoring it elsewhere.

Foreword

To offer these points is to say again that Krueger's probing book is provocative in good ways which can stimulate thought, push readers outside assumed categories, and (best of all) encourage readers to imagine a future better than our present. It is time for us to ease up substantially on our preoccupations with individual rights, however we define them. Indeed, what if we imposed a moratorium on talking about rights and on our practice of routinely translating questions about the common good into matters of individual entitlement? If Krueger's old-new conservatism in fact rises up to dominance, he will quite likely be right: the environmental cause will gain greater support and our lands and bodies will be better for it. But the resulting benefits would be more expansive than that, which is to say that Krueger's hopes seem ambitious indeed.

Preface

AN ADDICTED MAN HAS little reason to decry drunkenness until his ailing liver, his overdrawn accounts, or his estranged wife lead him to close the barroom door behind him for the final time. Outside in the quiet night, a bolted door behind him and as yet no open doors ahead, he must smash his treasured bottle with its amatory allure upon the gravel of his own brokenness, his own deficiency, his own suffering, all of which will indeed be his salvation if he persists. He must shatter one thing so that he might be whole. He must withdraw himself from one object, in order to restore communion with another. The everyday American, going about his business half-drugged by the endless assaults and seductive posturing of advertisers, media genies, and sham prophets of progress and productivity—his cords of addiction spread far and wide—cannot have anything of value to say of his own culture until he, too, steps away from his treasured amenities that nevertheless may be killing him. Anyone who would offer a robust assessment of his society must volunteer him- or herself to a sideline to watch the strange spectacle of that society with some measure of detachment.

In addition, because the environmentalist (along with the religious person) agrees that, despite the tremendous good that rarely fails to well up when human beings gather in common purpose, human society as it stands is nevertheless somehow broken, somehow prone to corruption, somehow inclined to mutiny against larger contexts that would remind it of its limitations. Therefore, the environmentalist, as with the religious person (if he would be worth his salt), is doubly called to make a break from the social order—a break not only with visible things or with the outward forms of society, but chiefly with the buried value structures and assumptions that undergird it. The whole vision of both the environmentalist and the religious person must be cleansed, that they may speak to their people with true vision.

Preface

Nature cannot be protected, honored, cared for, loved, participated in from within a system of values that scrape against her. Many of the values and standards forming the normative fibers of American liberal thought grow out of an inherent disdain for the routine limitations of nature (perhaps in part the strange fruits of an orchard planted in the restless city and not in quiet fields) and such value structures only work in the end to destroy and disfigure her. Since to love is to offer oneself for the sake of the other, authentic love for nature would express itself in sacrifice. The ease and predictability of an engineered environment, and elitist fantasies of leisure unwed to labor; the immediate gratification of every whim, and being waited on at the press of a button—an encounter with raw nature puts a swift end to these. In boiling life down to the basics, little room remains for the adolescent amplification of personal predilections and the positivistic but (in the end) perennially discontented and insubordinate spirit of progressivism that now appears to be the bedrock of popular liberal thinking. Certainly, an authentic love for nature would require their swift sacrifice. These do not stand much better in the contexts of any authentic relationship, be it a marriage, a family, or a community—especially when such a relationship is lived in conscious acknowledgment of the bonds by which it subsists, intergenerational bonds not only with the living, but with the dead and with those yet to come. Real relationships, real communion, real belonging is limiting to individualistic tendencies, which is why relationships on every level are faltering in our day and age: we simply refuse to surrender to their constraints. But the alternative to these constraints, it seems to me, is not any better. Indeed, it is far worse. The alternative is a world of self-seekers, constantly vying for the kill. It is a world of incessant clamor, disaffection, atomization, faithlessness, exploitation—a spiritual and environmental nightmare. We cannot have communion without limitation and surrender, and we cannot in turn have conservation without communion.

It betrays the very laws of nature to think that we can have it all. Global citizenry is no citizenry. Our best hope is to have one thing fully, our best intention to care for one place well. As it now stands, the environmental movement is undermined not mainly by its opponents, but by itself. It is undermined by a confusion of political language, a confusion that leads us to think that earth-care is somehow congruent with a liberal, progressivist agenda when the task at hand is anything but expansive and progressive, but is rather conservative. Today's environmental movement is undermined also by its refusal to volunteer itself to the sidelines of contemporary

Preface

American culture, and from there to offer an incisive critique of that culture. It cannot issue a call to greatness when it is unwilling to embrace for itself a courageous moral vision that is as outwardly honorable as it is internally coherent, a vision received in the place from whence all true prophets come—the bareness, the routine simplicity, of the wilderness.

We may here understand wilderness broadly or even metaphorically, as the place that is least propitious to our egocentric lives; the place that at once reveals the minuteness of our atomized selves and the steadfast solidity of that in which these little selves reside. Settled, domestic life is very much a wilderness in this sense, where we discover our belonging to the larger contexts of family, community, and land only to the degree that we also discover the dead ends of self-absorption. The limitations of self-expression inherent in peaceable domestic life, marriage, communal integrity, and husbandry of the land are in harmony with the prophet's wilderness, and the prophet's wilderness, in any case, is not a wilderness cut off from, or in some romanticized opposition to, human culture. The prophet's wilderness is the wilderness that surrounds human culture and gives it definition, for the prophet's concern is ultimately the health of his or her own people; a health best assessed by the givenness of creation's robust but stable fellowship, in which human culture partakes according to the unique characteristics of the human kind. Unless the prophet considers the lilies of the field and the birds of the air, he cannot properly consider his fellow men.[1] All religious accounts, and so all traditional moral and ethical frameworks, begin with the account of creation. Man finds no place except within the broader household of nature.

The Disfiguration of Nature is my small offering to help in these tasks; the tasks, that is, of cultural critique and the reestablishment of human culture within an ordered and given cosmos, and one that imposes real limitations upon our lives and desires. Such is a cosmos that demands our fidelity and is worthy of it, and presents us (in the end) with little choice in the matter. This book is, at the same time, an invitation to disconnection. Particularly, it is an invitation to disconnect from destructive illusions about both nature and ourselves in favor of a humble yet constructive—and eventually powerful—understanding, the kind that can create a desperately-needed common ground in service not only of our shared American landscape, but of the promise of sound and peaceable human culture upon it.

---

1. See Matt 6:25–34; Luke 12:22–31.

Preface

A NOTE ON TERMS

Though there are some good arguments for distinction, which are explained in the introduction, throughout this work I use "conservation" and "environmentalism" and their related terms synonymously. Similarly, I tend to use the term "land" in its broadest sense, to include not only its inorganic and inanimate features such as terrain, water, and sky, but also flora and fauna, including human life.

A NOTE ON READING THIS BOOK

I have intended that this book be read linearly from cover to cover. I am especially concerned that readers consider the chapters on abortion and LGBT narratives within the larger context of the work. Whether or not the reader ultimately agrees with all of my points, what is surveyed prior to and following these chapters will help him or her to understand better why I make them, and indeed why these chapters are included in this book at all.

Acknowledgements

We do no work in isolation, and no achievement belongs to single persons. A cursory attempt to tally the inputs of any undertaking, or even of a day of pure leisure, reveals to us that the debts we owe are enormous. It is easier, therefore, or at least more efficient, to take the credit ourselves, or to bestow it on a few select others. As far as this little book is concerned, little credit is due the author, who has merely done a bit of reporting. This work, though a provocative critique of American culture and politics offered in no uncertain terms, is yet at its heart a testimony from lonely, quiet places. I am chiefly indebted to these places. May they persist and flourish; may they be fruitful and multiply; may they be sheltered from the noise and violent progressivism of nearsighted enterprise.

I am secondarily indebted to my wife Maureen, whose gentle spirit, considered critique, and red pen have helped smooth the rougher tendencies of my thoughts, my sentiments, and my prose.

Thirdly, I am indebted to Eric T. Freyfogle, whose work has been an inspiration, whose feedback has been critical, and whose willingness to generously provide his thoughtful foreword has imparted to this work a dignity and roundness that I could not impart to it alone.

"Glory be to God on high, and on earth peace, good will towards men."
—Gloria in excelsis Deo[1]

Old Forge, NY, the Eve of Pentecost, 2018.

---

1. An ancient eucharistic hymn based on Luke 2:14.

Introduction

THE DAY IS RAW and gray, and the large hemlocks that encircle the house become animated only by the occasional gust of wind. When the breeze has passed, they duly settle back into their quiet contemplations. Though the fall is still on, it is growing older. Though the fall has indeed grown old, the winter steps forward, young and spirited. Already a mantle of snow covers the forests and the fields. Each day I peer out the windows, expectantly looking for the deer. They will soon be arriving from the ridges to browse in the thick evergreens of the river valley. The turkeys, on the other hand, have already changed their autumnal courses for winter routines. They are no longer seen in the late afternoons shyly slipping by under the protection of these sheltering trees as they forage from clearing to clearing and come to the water to drink. They will be scratching in the snow, content with whatever small morsels they may uncover there. As for us, we have been stacking and splitting wood for months, and will continue the day-long vigils of feeding the stoves for some time to come. The day is raw and grey, but the night has brought a bright, new snow. When summer comes again, the mountain springs and rills will run boldly and clearly because of this. O, the boring traditions that keep us well! O, the changeless change in these hills! The day is raw and grey, the fires are lit, and all is indeed well.

THE CONSERVATIVE ROOTS OF ENVIRONMENTAL ACTION

We tend to equate the environmental movement with the uproar and social upheaval of the 1960s. When the sixties came along, however, the environmental movement had a well-established and venerable history both in America and abroad. It is a history that, in surprising ways, challenges the now conventional notion that environmental conservation belongs to the liberal Democratic agenda. In fact, to this day, the American president who remains the national icon for farsighted conservation efforts is the larger-than-life Republican Theodore Roosevelt. By the time Roosevelt's two presidential terms were through in 1909, the avid outdoorsman and sportsman had created the United States Forest Service (USFS) and had established 150 national forests, fifty-one federal bird reserves (now national wildlife preserves), four national game preserves, five national parks, and eighteen national monuments. He protected approximately 230 million acres of public land as one of his top presidential priorities.[1] Emma Bryce, a blogger for the New York Times, cites a study that asked twelve leading environmental groups to name three presidents who, in their estimation, did the greatest good for the environment while in office. Teddy Roosevelt and Richard Nixon (yes, you read it right, Richard Nixon) come in first and second respectively as the top conservationist presidents of all time. The centrist Christian Democrat Jimmy Carter ranked third.[2]

There is further historical evidence that would challenge our notions about the roots and goals of the conservation movement. For one, it was the Republican Party, and not the Democratic Party, that was the forerunner in progressivism. By and large, progressivism meant the throwing off of traditional restraints in order to expand human enterprise and industry. Progressivism today—now in the popular mind belonging to the once conservative Democratic Party—is still very much driven by these same ambitions; with, perhaps, an even greater emphasis on social engineering than on industrial engineering, though the two are coincident. In its plucky youth, the call for conservation represented a conservative rejoinder to this progressive expansionism. The conservative voices of conservation sought to challenge the industrial outlook and its effect on the human spirit. They strove to check industrial expansion, especially when it imposed itself in corrosive ways on the land and on the people settled there. At the least, they sought to coordinate industrial endeavors when the conglomerates that carried them out proved unable to regulate themselves, either out of greed or because they were operating too provincially and were thus neglecting larger considerations. Roosevelt, though a progressive Republican, was nonetheless unafraid to speak out against the prevailing spirit of his time in order to contain the corporate conglomerates whose activities threatened

---

1. "Theodore Roosevelt," para. 4.
2. Bryce, "America's Greenest Presidents," fig. 1.

our national resources. For an example, in his December 3, 1907 State of the Union Address, he affirmed that

> The fortunes amassed through corporate organization are now so large, and vest such power in those that wield them, as to make it a matter of necessity to give to the sovereign—that is, to the Government, which represents the people as a whole—some effective power of supervision over their corporate use. In order to insure a healthy social and industrial life, every big corporation should be held responsible by, and be accountable to, some sovereign strong enough to control its conduct. I am in no sense hostile to corporations. This is an age of combination, and any effort to prevent all combination will be not only useless, but in the end vicious, because of the contempt for law which the failure to enforce law inevitably produces. We should, moreover, recognize in cordial and ample fashion the immense good effected by corporate agencies in a country such as ours, and the wealth of intellect, energy, and fidelity devoted to their service, and therefore normally to the service of the public, by their officers and directors. The corporation has come to stay, just as the trade union has come to stay. Each can do and has done great good. Each should be favored so long as it does good. But each should be sharply checked where it acts against law and justice.[3]

In his striving to check corporate expansion where he deemed necessary, Roosevelt was not being a revolutionary; he was not out to forge a brave new world. Rather, he conservatively sought to preserve something of the old world against the revolutionary tide of economic and industrial extension, and this included its caustic extension into the moral and social standards of the people.

The conservation movement that flowered under Roosevelt's leadership represented a conservative reaction against unchecked industrial expansion, yet in many ways it also absorbed the progressive spirit of the age. For an example, it was thought that the applied sciences, turned toward the natural world, would allow for even greater yields of natural resources. To an extent, this proved true, but scientifically trained conservationists such as Aldo Leopold (d. 1949) would come to see the limitations of such an approach, reminding us that it would take more than applied science to keep our lands heathy. Rather, it would take a shift in values and cultural assumptions. We must turn away from the individualistic, expansionist

---

3. Roosevelt, "Seventh Annual Message," para. 5.

attitudes that have driven and have come to dominate the industrial age, turning instead toward a more quotidian and settled respect for the land and our duties upon it. In the pages of American literature, such a call comes perhaps most incisively and presciently not from the Progressive North, but from the pens of twelve Southern conservatives.

First published in 1930, *I'll Take My Stand: The South and the Agrarian Tradition* not only fundamentally challenges the idea that environmentalism is a leftist, liberal cause, but will also challenge common perspectives about the Civil War and the underlying social and political visions that were at stake therein. I am a Northern Yankee proud of his New England blood, suckled on the pondering transcendentalism of writers such as Emerson and Thoreau and triumphalist and oversimplified Northern versions of Civil War history. From the perspective of these twelve southern agrarians, however, the American Civil War was not so much a conflict between abolitionist and pro-slavery parties as a struggle between an expansionist, industrializing, urbanizing North and a provincial, agrarian South. In other words, as has been the case since the beginning of the Industrial Revolution, the Civil War, among other things, presents another occasion where restless, progressive industry prevailed over a society more apt to settle. The South was not merely protecting the institution of slavery, but an economy and a way of life that was, at its heart, agrarian. Indeed, the grime and overcrowding of the Northern cities provided Southerners with little reason to envy them. One contributor even highlights the tendency of industrialization to amplify race tensions rather than to subdue them, and holds out the promise of rural, small-town, agrarian life as the best way, however slow it may be, to authentic conciliation.[4] Though it would be hard to take the proud Yankee out of me, the discovery of *I'll Take My Stand* has turned my world upside down. No serious environmentalist should go without reading it. "We have been taught," writes Andrew Nelson Lytle, one of the book's contributors, "by Jefferson's struggles with Hamilton, by Calhoun's with Webster, and in the woods at Shiloh or along the ravines of Fort Donelson where the long hunter's rifle spoke defiance to the more accelerated Springfields, that the triumph of industry, commerce, trade, brings misfortune to those who live on the land." Lytle continues,

> Since 1865 an agrarian Union has been changed into an industrial empire bent on conquest of the earth's goods and ports to sell them in. This means warfare, a struggle over markets, leading, in

---

4. Robert Penn Warren, "The Briar Patch," 246–64.

the end, to actual military conflict between nations. But, in the meantime, the terrific effort to manufacture ammunition—that is, wealth—so that imperialism may prevail, has brought upon the social body a more deadly conflict, one which promises to deprive it, not of life, but of living; take the concept of liberty from the political consciousness; and turn the pursuit of happiness into a nervous running-around which is without the logic, even, of a dog chasing its tail.[5]

TODAY'S MUDDLED ENVIRONMENTAL MOVEMENT

Though history jumbles the familiar categories a great deal, today nearly everyone with whom you will speak on both the Left and the Right will label conservation a liberal, progressive, Democratic cause. And because it has become the child of the Left, it has along the way inherited many political and social bedmates that serve to confuse and obscure its message—and not just for the general public, but within its own ranks. This essay seeks to untangle some of these liaisons, and perhaps even to inspire a much-needed farewell between the environmental cause and the muddled company it keeps.

The marriage of the conservation movement to a liberal agenda that has increasingly had the ear of various radical special interest groups has been one of the most disastrous political, social, and environmental pitfalls in recent times. Not only has it served to obscure the commonality of the conservationist cause, the fact that healthy lands benefit all of us, but it also has wedded conservation efforts with other agendas and narratives that remain unpalatable to many decent Americans. To give the knife another twist, these very narratives and agendas and the underlying value structures that support them denigrate rather than strengthen the very moral and ethical vision that would serve to sustain a robust conservationism. In other words, some of the core commitments of the current liberal agenda are at best incongruent with and at worst antithetical to the moral integrity and self-regulating attitude that is so necessary for a robust environmental ethic. Today we find the besmirched specter of an environmentalism prepackaged with ideologies that, at their heart, represent a disaffection from, and so disfiguration of, nature itself.

---

5. Lytle, "The Hind Tit," 202.

At the same time, many of the conservative values that are openly disdained by liberals are the very values that would shape a strong ethic of conservation if expanded along their natural lines to embrace such a commitment. These values include strong families and the local communities/governments/economies built upon them; personal integrity and morality; the begetting, safeguarding, and pedagogy of children for disciplined citizenship and the sustenance of culture and community; and stability in relationships and place, to include the subsequent maintenance of strong ties with the past and with one's cultural and religious roots that come with such a commitment to stability. An esteem for rural life lived close to the land in honest and disciplined productivity is another necessary ingredient to a conservationism that would be true to itself. This necessarily includes a love of sport in the wilderness, such as hunting, fishing, and trapping. Make no bones about it: conservation is conservative and commonsensical. Eric T. Freyfogle, the Max L. Row Professor of Law at the University of Illinois College of Law, argues in his book, *Why Conservation is Failing and How It Can Regain Ground*, that organized conservation, when it first gained momentum over a century ago, "was less liberal than society as a whole."[6]

The terms conservative and liberal are perhaps two of the most misused words in our time. The result of their misuse is public and political confusion. Conservatism as an ideology, writes environmental educator C. A. Bowers, "represents a tradition of thinking about the most fundamental relationships within communities (and cultures)."[7] Edmund Burke

---

6. Freyfogle, *Why Conservation is Failing*, 7.

7. Bowers, *Mindful Conservatism*, 9. Bowers's book goes a long way in helping to establish the conservativism that must stand behind a sound environmental ethic. Throughout, he argues strongly for the maintenance and integrity of traditional linguistic and cultural systems that help to foster cohesion among various peoples, connecting them to their environment and to one another in non-monetary, non-consumeristic ways, and providing moral limitations on their behavior within the broader contexts of their lives, both social and environmental. The book, however, ultimately disappoints when one finds him, in the end, furthering the very same liberal agenda that he so sharply criticizes throughout the work. He does this by an unexamined, unexplained, and unwarranted dismissal of the book of Genesis as if it were the root of all Western evils, notably an attitude of anthropocentrism. Not only does he not consider Genesis within its context (the whole of the biblical canon as well as the living interpretative and practical traditions that draw out its subtle meanings), but he also dismisses with the same brush of his hand a powerful mytho-poetic narrative that would serve to put man in his place both physically and morally. Indeed, the first eleven chapters of Genesis remind us again and again that we are only finite creatures, not gods, and that the limitations imposed on our lives by God and the created order itself, though perhaps frustrating, are also limitations on

(1729–1797) is commonly considered to be the founder of modern philosophical conservatism. Reflecting on the French Revolution, Burke believed that reforms "should be based on the experience of the community rather than on abstract ideas—which are usually formulated by theorists who are outsiders. Changes are thus to be assessed in terms of whether they contribute to the further well-being of the community."[8] Burke also believed that change needs to be assessed not by what is convenient only for the living, but out of the understanding that we are in "a partnership between those who are living, those who are dead, and those who are to be born."[9] The past and the future both matter as much as the present: past, present, and future are one continuum. Our decisions and actions, and how we pursue or refuse change, must be measured by criteria that extend beyond our own personal ambitions, desires, conveniences, profits, and lifetimes. Conservatism, then, is not in keeping with a liberal agenda of unchecked, present-day gains at the expense of traditional cultures and the places that shape these cultures, or of the past, or of the generations who are to come. Liberalism, the ideology very much behind globalization, tends otherwise, relying on the myth of progress to justify its near total disregard for tradition, culture, community, and the land itself. This attack is waged through the relentless pursuit of private autonomy, the maximization of individual choice over communal considerations, technological innovation, and the drive to expand markets and profits. The limitation of government, both on local and national levels, is part and parcel to this agenda, which not only undermines the democratic process, but routs the ability of communities to protect themselves and to conserve that which makes them unique, such

---

the amount of evil we could and would otherwise do without these constraints. Far from being a cheeky celebration of man's dominance, Genesis is rather a record of the depth of his fall. Despite its dismissal by the politically correct, educated secularists of our time— and generally not only because of its affirmation of human dominion but also ironically because of its insistence that humanity is bound to obedience to a higher order—Genesis continues to shape subcultures in the West in positive ways. Such sub-cultures strive to maintain, against all odds, their own traditional linguistic and cultural systems that help them to foster cohesion and true community, that connect them to their environment (God's good creation) and one another in non-monetary, non-consumeristic ways, and that encode a hierarchy of values that would limit and inform their interactions with one another and with nature. From the Amish to monastic communities, this literature has shown its power to undergird the kinds of communities that Bowers finds so necessary for resisting patterns of global consumption.

8. Bowers, *Mindful Conservatism*, 10.
9. Quoted in Bowers, *Mindful Conservatism*, 10.

as cultural traditions, skills, local economies (monetarily based and otherwise), and land resources.

As mentioned above, we have to remember that the Republican Party was once the forerunner in progressivism, while the Democrats were the conservative group. This is the opposite of what we generally think today. But today's labels emerge from a mistaken perception, for we have not only lost track of the history of the two parties, but of the history of ideas themselves, especially of what liberalism and conservatism actually are. Today, many so-called conservative Republicans are actually libertarians in sheep's clothing. They advance the same industrializing, big business agendas as they advanced (according to many) in Civil War times, couching this liberal, progressive agenda of unchecked global enterprise in the pleasing rhetoric of family values and making America great again. But the meat of their platform is liberal, equally radical and destructive of stable society as the other liberal agendas forwarded by the radical Left. As has been said, the conservation movement was by and large conservative. It relied heavily on strong governmental leadership, seeking to limit human endeavor, not to expand it. It also appealed to a sense of decency, personal moral integrity, and an outlook where larger considerations tempered the sense of individual rights and privileges.

In any case, both Republican and Democratic presidents furthered the conservationist cause.[10] Both parties advanced federal interventions to make necessary corrections to some of the pressing problems of the age. These problems included industrialization, urbanization, immigration, corporate monopolies, corruption in government, an overzealous and nearsighted individualism, and their attendant overconsumption of resources and spoil to the natural environment. The role of both parties in advancing such interventions in part demonstrates the shades of grey inherent in black and white terms such as "conservative" and "liberal," while also revealing the bullheadedness of believing that certain issues and solutions belong solely to either one political party or another. Party politics need not be perpetual warfare simply for the sake of some meaningless market competition. We are not, in the end, opponents, but must work together

---

10. The Progressive-era conservation movement is often considered to span the presidencies of Theodore Roosevelt, William Howard Taft, and Woodrow Wilson (1901–1921). The former two were Republicans, while the latter was a Democrat. The ground for the movement, however, was prepared long before this time. Samuel P. Hays, in his seminal historical account of the Progressive-era conservation movement entitled *Conservation and the Gospel of Efficiency*, covers the three decades between 1890 and 1920.

to find the greatest goods shared by most. The integrity of the land—for pleasure, health, productivity, and posterity—is one of the most palpable of these goods.

Nevertheless, it remains true that many of the values that we now label "traditional" or that fall under a correct usage of the word "conservative" are precisely the values that would, when brought to their logical ends, bolster a strong conservation ethic. At the same time, many of the values that have driven the agendas of the Left, when brought to their logical ends, prove not only to be incongruent with, but devastating to, a strong conservation ethic. It is these values more than the trendy or politically correct beliefs that we express (such as, "it is good to care for the environment") that will ultimately shape what we do. These values will serve to give definition (or lack thereof) to a society that will have what it takes—the personal and communal integrity, the emotional maturity, the physical endurance, and the right moral reasoning—to conserve its resources for future generations.

Though many opportunities for conservation are missed when we focus our debates too heavily on the role of the federal government—indeed, efforts that are localized to state, county, municipality, and grassroots levels can make for powerful programs that can yet be responsive to local needs while empowering local people—the conservatism necessary to accomplish and inspire effective conservation efforts throughout the union will require clear, strong, courageous governmental leadership on every level. This naturally includes a federal level. The idea that clarity of federal leadership is essential for the integrity of the union was, after all, the founding insight of the Republican Party from Lincoln right up through the Progressive-era conservation movement. All complex projects need a master plan, and it is at the federal level where such planning and implementation must take place. It is a libertarian, and not a classically conservative, stance that seeks to deregulate most everything and leave government stripped of its power to help guide and, well, govern a people. We should know the difference between the two. Libertarianism forgets that all organic bodies—including communal bodies—need integrity, definition, and regulation in order to survive. An indispensable part of this integrity is a strong immune system and a clear head, if for nothing else than to protect against the viral and cancerous members who cannot self-regulate and who consistently impinge and profit on others without regard to the health of the whole.

Conserving resources in our time will indeed take great moral strength, integrity, and clarity of leadership. We will be called to lessen our commitments to comfort, convenience, connectivity, mobility, a high-minded cosmopolitanism, and radicalized special interests. Because this is the case, it is unlikely that either a revolutionary spirit or an urban, cosmopolitan experience will lead to a viable ethic of conservation. Rather, the conservation ethic belongs to the spare routineness of rural and small-town experience, an experience that is very much undervalued, if not despised and marginalized, in our time. It is undervalued both from within and from without, so much so that the rural and small-town experience, and the values that this experience shapes and that shape it, are in danger of near total extinction. Such a devaluation is not only to be seen in the methods and means of the factory farm and the strip mine, but also in the proliferation of wind farms on wooded ridges, and solar farms in fields that once produced both food and fuel. All of these serve to transform rural landscapes into industrial ones. Because conservation is of nature and concerned with nature, its realization demands a closeness and obedience to nature's limitations. Those who would conserve are not called to reinvent the world, nor to save it through technological mastery or social revolution, but by obedience to nature. We are called to plant our roots in a place, which includes the human community of that place, and to live in harmony with that place and the people who share it for better and for worse, for richer and for poorer, in sickness and in health. In short, conservation demands a very real conservatism. It demands self-regulation and a commitment to allow one's own boundaries to be dictated, in part, by the limitations imposed by an "other" with whom we are in relationship. In this case, both the land and the people with whom we exist as part of that land—the dead, the living, and those yet to come—comprise that "other." When we cannot live with this kind of humble obedience to other, when self-regulation is subjugated by self-indulgence, then not only human community, but nature itself, will be disclaimed and disfigured.

THE DISFIGURATION OF NATURE: THE BURDEN OF THIS ESSAY

In the event that my words are misleading, let it be clearly stated that the disfiguration of nature, which is the burden of this essay, is perpetrated from all places and all sides. We are all involved in the problem. Those who we currently call "conservatives" and "liberals" alike have bloodied hands. If so-called conservatives were half as committed to the values they often like to espouse, they would deeply question and seek to check corporate greed and power (as the Republicans once did), the vacuity of consumerism, genetic engineering's attack on natural order and the integrity of species (an attack akin to the liberal social engineer's campaign against the integrity of the family), a wanton love of weapons, and a host of other allegiances that in one way or another wage war on stable society and an obedience to the limitations of nature. These limitations are yet the very same natural constraints that such people would rightly evoke when criticizing various LGBTQ narratives, the defacement of marriage and the family, Planned Parenthood and its empire of abortion and contraception, and so on. This disfiguration of nature seems to be the product of an increasing disaffection from nature itself, a disaffection that is bipartisan and has left us confused and unable to find solid ground. To lose one's grip on reality is traditionally called insanity, though I hear it called many things, such as "courage" or "creativity," "progress" or perhaps "following one's own truth." Call it what you will, it is still a sickness and an error, and this sickness now darkens the conceptions of mankind. Nature is objective, and if we are to be in right relationship with her, then we must be limited by the reality that she imposes on us. Humility and sacrifice are, as they ever shall be, our only sane way forward.

Though not intended to be an historical study per se, but rather an ethical one, this short piece will begin with a general and terse historical exploration of the values and socio-political factors that have shaped and inspired the conservation movement in America. It will do this in order to trace the almost imperceptible shift this movement has taken from common cause, conservative in the classical sense, to leftist radicalism, at least in public opinion. Because, politically speaking, the movement belongs to the Left, the environmental cause has been wedded to other causes that have made it opaque and unpalatable to many American people. We will look at the most notorious of these causes, enquiring into the leading ideas that drive them and the underlying moral and ethical worldviews that shape them in an effort to discern their congruity with the ethics that would support stout conservation efforts. It will be demonstrated that, while many of these agendas may stem from well-meaning motivations, a number of them serve only to distract, divide, and so gridlock forward movement for conservation. Yet other agendas will be shown to be downright antithetical in the end to the values that would best bolster a robust environmentalism. Such agendas will include narratives about gender, abortion, family, and economics, right down to the underlying anthropology—that is, the perception of the human person herself—that inspires and feeds these narratives.

Taking a similar tack, we will then look at what I will call (with some poetic-license, I realize) conservative, rural values and relate these to an ecosystem of personal and communal commitments that might bolster and inspire a full-bodied and much-needed conservation ethic in America. Such an ethic, as it did in its infancy, would clothe the American soul with decency and integrity, and serve to make the common person proud. Further than this, I hope to demonstrate that the conservation and environmental cause is not only common to both liberals and conservatives, but that it actually (and perhaps startlingly) fits better within a framework that is creatively conservative than in one that is radically liberal. Indeed, those who would inherit the earth are those who would live meekly on and with it, not those who would forge their identities on constant revolt and change for the sake of change.

This work is by no means intended to be an uncritical endorsement of conservatism, even less of what we colloquially but mistakenly call conservative. As I have already stated, the GOP can hardly be called conservative. Historically, it was the progressive party. Today, it tends toward the libertarian, and this has been the case since at least the Reagan Era. Our most recent election has proven in a stark way how far the GOP has fallen. To be honest, for most of my life I have been a Democrat. These commitments have largely to do with the Democratic Party's loyalties to robust social supports and to the environment. I have, however, grown increasingly aware of, and troubled by, the extremism and fundamentalism of the liberal agenda, not to mention its descent into capriciousness. The phenomenon is not unique to the Democrats, and as public discourse now stands, the terms "conservative" and "liberal" are entirely misleading. It is a liberal conservatism, or even a conservative liberalism, that serves as the founding DNA of both American life and the American conservation effort, and the problems of our age cross all party lines; they belong to all of us. On all sides, there is confusion about the goods and evils, the pleasures and pains, the comforts and threats, of globalism, a consistently revolutionizing force that is inherently destructive of local communities, cultures, and economies. On all sides, there is confusion about the technological juggernaut, its possibilities for good and for ill, its responsible uses and its misuses, its service to humanity or its enslavement of humanity, and its potential to render the world unrecognizable from one generation to another and so to sever the necessary intergenerational relationships that form stable societies and cultures. We must contend with forces that seek to sever our connections to our past, forces that haphazardly and even maliciously engineer some brave new society, consistently throwing out the proverbial baby with the bathwater. In short, the American people are confounded by complexity on every side; is it any wonder that, on all sides, we seem to be retreating into our various ghettos?

Because we all, on the Left and the Right, make the same fallacious and unexamined assumptions, especially when it comes to the nature of rights, we find ourselves locked in a constant clash where one individual's right impedes upon another's. Such warfare is the only possible outcome for a society of atomized individuals. We cannot see beyond the individual, to the dependencies and conditions that give him or her life, and so are unable to perceive a way forward and to work together for the things that affect and connect most of us the most. The land is the greatest of these things. The land, being the very reality on and in which we dwell and upon which our lives and wealth depend, can have a great, simplifying immediacy. Our inability to step up together to acknowledge the land, and then to care for it in a way that is consistent with the reality it presents to us, not only bears witness to the troubling emotional regression of our times and its resultant disorientation, but also to the tallness of the task itself. That task requires us to hold fast against the inertia and the intensity of the forces that would distract us from maintaining with integrity our connection to and care for place. We must hold fast against a veritable onslaught of glittering but pernicious promises. Surprisingly (to many of my friends, but perhaps mostly to myself) I am coming to believe that conservatives, if true to many of the core values that once united them, if true to classical conservatism, are the ones who will be best equipped by these very same values to face the tall task at hand. Liberals have become too weakened and distracted by enforcing political correctness and upholding special interest causes that are, in the end, not only morally abhorrent to many Americans, but that also are incongruent with conservationist values themselves.

Once again, this is not to say that Republicans are not equally distracted. These supposed conservatives suffer from the same party fundamentalism and petty commitments to special interest groups as do Democrats. They, too, do obeisance to the immoral, to the money, and to the emotionally weak rather than to stand true to the values that inspire true conservatism. What is more, today's so-called "conservatives" are prone to the same muddling of categories that has caused so much political, social, and moral confusion in our time, thinking that they are being conservative while actually promoting liberalism and libertarianism. True conservatives, therefore, must be willing to take a stand for their traditional values against forces such as big corporations and the unchecked expansion of the market mentality into all aspects of life. They must be willing also to loosen their hold on a few pet issues (the proliferation of weapons, for an example)[11] that serve only to divide and distract the American public from the real tasks at hand. The conservationist cause belongs to the same value systems that would forward a pro-life, pro-family commitment. These must be the rationale behind, as they are the outcome of, right relationship with nature. This work is, therefore, every bit as much a challenge to conservatives as it is to liberals. The challenge is to shake off the dubious and radical libertarianism that has so thoroughly infected their thinking. The challenge is to loosen the shackles of their enslavement to big business, to curb the childish demand for total freedom in the markets, and to return to their roots. Those who value family and a child in the womb should know above all that not everything can be determined by the market, and that not everything that the market determines is good. Children, stable marriages, strong local governments and economies, a productive life on productive land—we do not measure the value of these by what price they can bring us in the marketplace. Conservatives must gather themselves in to a sound and decent morality that embraces what is good and wholesome, what is middle and working class, what is of the land; a morality that honors civility, truth, virtue, sacrifice, discipline, and so limitation, and then expand these values to their dealings with the land. This would make for conservationism at its finest.

In short, I am not herein endorsing any political party as each now stands. Rather, in this work I hope to provide some food for thought for people of all political persuasions and commitments who wish to sort out

11. I realize that the issue at stake with gun ownership does not always stem from an abhorrent love of weaponry, but from considerations of constitutional freedoms and rights. As we will see in chapter 2, our basic assumptions about rights are very often wrong. Even if the right to bear arms pertained to atomized individuals without regard for the common good, I would argue that it is a right worth trading in order to save the lives of millions of unborn children, for one example. It is hard to cry murder in the case of abortion and in the next breath defend an unstable, perhaps already criminally convicted person's "right" to procure assault weapons, especially in the wake of yet another massacre of children in our schools. See footnote 10 in chapter 7.

and get clearer on one of the more pressing issues of our day. I hope to achieve this by breaking environmentalism and conservation away from their current bedmate issues that serve to sour them for so many people. This is helpful for two reasons. First, that we might be able to appreciate conservation on its own terms, and so drill down into the moral and ethical commitments that would best undergird it. Secondly, that we might be able to assess whether the arguments and worldviews that undergird these other issues are congruent with the moral and ethical commitments necessary to further the conservationist cause, or if they rather detract from and undermine them. Relating these worldviews to the issue of conservation, we will begin to identify what value structures would best fortify a strong environmental ethic, an ethic that will look surprisingly conservative in the classical and true sense of that term. Such an exercise will go a long way in helping us to forge a necessary future as one of the world's most powerful and wealthy nations, that we might unite (or inch closer together) in a rounded, wholesome, and authentically American response to the imperatives of our time.

May we come to perceive creative ways into the future that need not dishonor our bodies, our natures, and our ancestors; one that honors the land that has fed our forefathers and mothers, that has shaped their values and educated them in a productive conservatism, and that has, in the last, taken them into itself.

Chapter 1

Conservation: A Brief History

The nations raged, but your wrath came,
 and the time for the dead to be judged,
for rewarding your servants, the prophets and saints,
 and those who fear your Name, both small and great,
and for destroying the destroyers of the earth.

—Rev 11:18

JOHN MUIR, THE MODERATELY rebellious and certainly unconventional self-made botanist and geographer of Yosemite, was visited by Theodore Roosevelt in 1903. Roosevelt was entering his third year as president, having risen to the post after the assassination of William McKinley, and he was Muir's junior by twenty years. Not long after the two met, the larger-than-life president's exuberance for adventure and sport won him a friendly chastisement from the quiet, peaceable Muir.

"Mr. Roosevelt," said he; "when are you going to get beyond the boyishness of killing things? Are you not getting far enough along to leave that off?"

Roosevelt's entourage of fawning bootlickers fell silent, nearly falling over.

"Muir, I guess you're right," Roosevelt replied obligingly.

As the story goes, Roosevelt went a-hunting regardless, though only out of sheer duty: his stated intent was to collect museum specimens for educational purposes.[1]

Many years earlier, in 1871, Muir was visited by the bookish essayist and poet Ralph Waldo Emerson. The two quickly became fast friends, and Muir urged him to come away with him to camp in the wilderness. Emerson was getting on in age, and his own fawning entourage would not allow this. Roosevelt, however, had no such reservations. He was, in fact, determined to camp despite the five feet of spring snow that lay on the ground in many places. The two men, one a quiet lover of nature and the other a boisterous and manly lover of sport, went forth together into the American wilderness that so wholly sparked their shared zest for life. They spent the first night at Mariposa Grove under the Grizzly Giant, and the second night in the vicinity of Sentinel Dome.[2]

"Bully!" exclaimed the President repeatedly as he admired the grand landscape. When the two woke to five inches of new snow on top of that which was already on the ground, Roosevelt yowled, "This is bullier yet! I wouldn't miss this for the world!"

As they huddled around the warming campfires each evening, Muir had the president's ear. Indeed, the president was more than willing to offer it. Their respective personalities were in many ways vastly different, and yet they shared much common ground. Their mutual love for the beauty of the American landscapes, their desire to preserve our natural resources, and their willingness to make bold stands and generous sacrifices to honor and protect them united the two men. Roosevelt wrote a lovely tribute to John Muir that was published in *The Outlook* magazine, of which Roosevelt was an associate editor, in 1915. He stated that Muir "was a great factor in influencing the thought of California and the thought of the entire country so as to secure the preservation of those great natural phenomena—wonderful canyons, giant trees, slopes of flower-spangled hillsides—which make California a veritable Garden of the Lord."[3]

Under the presidency of Theodore Roosevelt, the conservation movement would come to full flower in the realm of federal public policy. This may lead us to believe that environmental protection belongs to the modern progressive. But the movement itself was by no means something

---

1. Heacox, *Visions of a Wild America*, 29.
2. "Theodore Roosevelt," para. 2.
3. Roosevelt, "John Muir," 27–28.

novel. In every age of Western civilization and beyond, the imperative for conservation of natural resources has been recognized and articulated. In America, astute farmers were already taking first steps toward an American conservationism in the early 1800s. James Madison, for an example, newly retired from his presidency, delivered a prescient speech to his local agricultural society in Albemarle County, Virginia in 1818. In his talk, Madison spoke of the farmer's association with the greater reality of nature. In order to build a strong republican nation, citizens needed to have a long view, and a long view would require each citizen to properly steward the land, giving back to it what one took. Madison cautioned against the lure of expansion for the sake of expansion, warning that this did not necessarily create wealth or signify progress.[4]

Figures such as Edmund Ruffin (1794–1865) would also hold high a similar torch. Perceiving with regret the telltale signs of poor land use, and deeply concerned about its social implications (for Ruffin's case especially in the Antebellum South), Ruffin urged fellow farmers to conserve and to cycle nutrients back into their soils through the use of cover crops and aged manure. Stephen Stoll's *Larding the Lean Earth* is a wonderful and important historical treatment of American soil and the early farmers who sought to protect and nurture it as it nurtured them. Speaking of Edmund Ruffin's South, Stoll writes, "throughout the 1830s and 1840s an out-migration on a scale never before seen in the United States raised the strange prospect that settled society in South Carolina might fail its mission."[5] Ruffin and others like him, in both the South and the North, tried to convince farmers to stay in their native east and care for their soils rather than wasting the land and then moving westward in order to find new property. Western land was abundant and cheap, but it was land that those moving onto it would eventually also use poorly and exhaust, as evidenced by the Dust Bowl years of the early 1930s. This distinctly American relationship with land—that one could use it up and move on, finding fertile land elsewhere rather easily and inexpensively—seems to have done much to form an American ethos. It is an ethos that still rumbles around today in the assumptions of a disposable, mobile culture that refuses to acknowledge limitation and is all too willing to forsake a homeland for prospects elsewhere. Indeed, every American of an ancestry other than Native American has in their family history the massive emotional complexity of emigration from a native land in order to

4. Stoll, *Larding the Lean Earth*, 37.
5. Stoll, *Larding the Lean Earth*, 122.

pursue opportunity in a foreign one. Ruffin, being a good farmer, knew the value of strong roots. Whatever brought his ancestors here, he was unwilling to throw his homeland away, and sought to find ways to reinvigorate that land and the people upon it through his efforts and experiments in soil management and improvement. An ardent secessionist who claimed to have fired the first shot of the Civil War at Fort Sumpter, Ruffin was indeed a complex historical figure, one that must be counted as a forefather of the American conservation movement and of modern soil science.

Speaking of "improving" farmers such as Ruffin, Stoll points out that "conservation is barely distinguishable from conservatism in these examples, according to their common root: to preserve from decay or loss, to maintain in continuous existence."[6] The values that motivated their efforts toward a more conscientious husbandry of the land included "responsibility, self-denial, ties to society through family, and the solemn transmittal of values and practices; social mobility by hard work, not greed; social order and leadership by respected elites, not demagogues; education, religion, and temperance in all things."[7]

Similarly, Richard Judd, in tracing the origins of conservation in Northern New England, finds its roots embedded in the soils of the small freeholder. Seeking to strike a balance between the utilitarian goals of human flourishing and productiveness with the republican values of common stewardship, democratic access to land resources, and a sense of embeddedness in the household of nature, early New Englanders developed a complex social system that served to check missteps in land use, abuses of land resources, and undue dominance over them. These social systems were deeply moral, sustained by tradition, favored communal needs over individual predilections, and so were naturally conservative.[8] Whether we are talking about ancient biblical literature or the romantic poems of Wordsworth, humans have always appreciated their tenuous place in the grand scheme of things. Conservative voices in every generation have articulated the need to restrict our taking and pay due service and homage to that which sustains our common lives and cultures. Equally in every age and every culture, a blind enthusiasm for limitless prosperity, the temptations to greed and wantonness, the rush of ambition and avarice, and the clamor of the perpetually dissatisfied and restive few have strived against

6. Stoll, *Larding the Lean Earth*, 89.
7. Stoll, *Larding the Lean Earth*, 90.
8. Judd, *Common Lands*.

a more quotidian, measured, far-sighted, disciplined self-restraint, a happy acceptance of limitation, a charitable contentment, and a frugal opulence.

The Industrial Revolution gave the conservation imperative a new urgency, and forced its playing field into the realm of state and federal policy. Markets expanded, and pressure from distant forces destabilized local networks of reciprocity and obligation. Beyond the pale of parochial adjustments and agreements, the activities of regionalized and nationalized conglomerates called for regionalized and nationalized checks and balances. The rapid advent of new technologies also contributed to the instability. They not only allowed for easier and more efficient means of resource exploitation and the relative ease of shipping those resources elsewhere (especially to the growing urban centers), but they also allowed for a certain distance between man and his environment, at least for some. A new spirit of possessive individualism was in the air, and in almost all instances excitement at the prospects won the day. Self-regulation gave way to self-assertion, which in turn contested community obligations. As local, land-based communal structures lost their integrity, so also the integrity of the land diminished.

A key characteristic of this frenetic industriousness was that it was haphazard, and therefore wasteful. Because there was no master plan or overall organizing structure to guide resource development and other land use practices, such practices tended to be inefficient and provincial. In the words of Samuel P. Hays, public policy became a means by which to transform a "loosely organized society, where waste and inefficiency ran rampant, into a highly organized, technical, and centrally planned and directed social organization which could meet a complex world with efficiency and purpose."[9] To replace such haphazard competition and its attendant wastefulness with centralized guidance and planning, far from halting or slowing economic development, would only create new heights of material abundance for the future, or at least a sustained yield. The self-regulating conservatism of the local communities was transferred to state and federal levels, becoming embedded in official policy.

As much as large-scale enterprise necessitated large-scale regulation, the latter was not without its incongruities. Richard Judd points out that, "as more aggressive urban elites took up the conservation crusade" toward the end of the nineteenth century and certainly in the beginning of the next,

---

9. Hays, *Gospel of Efficiency*, 265.

"the debate of the place of nature in the agrarian landscape faded."[10] Prior to this, long-term landowners' "relation to nature turned on a familiar sense of community responsibility and reverential respect for natural order."[11] One of the consequences of the more top-down approach forwarded in the Progressive Era—driven, as it tended to be, by bureaucrats and professional bests rather than from the grounded experience of everyday land users—was that landowners began to feel imposed upon from the outside. At the same time, many of these conservation laws favored urban users of the land, such as sport hunters and anglers, without regard to the needs of the local people. Judd suggests that Progressive-era conservationism "cast urban, elite champions of preservation against . . . petty resource users."[12] In our time, the portrait of the recalcitrant rural landowner in the face of environmental regulation borders on stereotype. He is largely a product of this period and of these forces, which continue to this day. The stereotype, however, is an incomplete portrait because, as has already been stated, the local landowner was the first to cry out against the exploitation of land resources by distant users, whose speculative activities either threatened or effectively denied communities of stable land users their ability to subsist.

Highlighting a similar, somewhat ironic disjuncture, Hays explains that federal and state forestry programs, by the sheer bulk of their bureaucratic substance, tended to expedite "large-scale corporate use of the forests"[13] while "subordinating the aesthetic to the utilitarian."[14] Despite the very real need for an overarching, unifying directive emanating from all levels of government, both to yoke otherwise self-interested constituencies with a larger vision and purpose and to rein in distant corporate occupation run riot, it would be a grave error to underestimate the role of small land users in the conservation effort, both historically and presently. Judd's study bears generous witness to the indispensable role that stable landowners, intimate with their place, must play in effective conservation. Referring to his travels in northern New England, Judd reflects in his preface,

> Time and again I encountered something akin to what Aldo Leopold called a land ethic among people . . . who considered themselves stewards of the farm they inherited and would pass on . . .

10. Quoted in Judd, *Common Lands*, 89.
11. Judd, *Common Lands*, 89.
12. Judd, *Common Lands*, 197.
13. Judd, *Common Lands*, 91.
14. Hays, *Gospel of Efficiency*, 127.

> [These encounters] suggested something that should have been obvious: second- or third-generation families, working their own soils, developed powerful attachments to a familiar landscape and to the natural dynamics that sustained it. This popular ethic was neither uniformly conservationist nor anticonservationist, as we define these terms today, but it was indeed a force to be reckoned with ... It inspired a penetrating search for the regularities and harmonies of nature, and it gave local land-use practices a definably moral cast.[15]

Many small land users embedded in communal and generational networks of mutual exchange, as opposed to a few big ones working from outside these networks, is the best insurance of liberty and responsible land use. Citing Harvard botanist Charles S. Sargent, Judd considers the invaluable part played by nineteenth-century private rural landowners in the forest stewardship of the time. "The real progress in silviculture in Massachusetts," wrote Sargent, "has been made by the farmers of Barnstable and Plymouth counties, who have taught us how to plant and raise forests successfully and profitably, under the most unfavorable conditions."[16] The Massachusetts farmers whom Sargent praises so highly would offset the functional concerns that attend agrarian life with the pietistic views of nature that life on the land and traditional rural values fashion. Judd demonstrates that farmers and small manufacturers, what he might call "petty resource users," were instrumental in the fight against absentee land speculators and corporate conglomerates whose uses of the land were driven by a profit motive stripped of the more quotidian and sobering considerations that discipline the pursuits of long-term residents on the land. Such commercial activities also served to remove the local resources on which communities depended in favor of distant markets. For forestry, this was especially the case with the struggle against the slash and burn practices of the pulp wood industry, but the story read the same with other resources. Speaking of fisheries, for an example, Judd sums up the situation this way: "Commercial fishing was less democratic and less responsive to community needs."[17] Today, I would make the same assertion about a certain breed of land speculator who stockpiles relatively inexpensive country properties and turns them into vacation rentals, or real estate brokers who consis-

15. Judd, *Common Lands*, xii.
16. Sargent was quoted in *Annual Report of the Secretary of the Massachusetts Board of Agriculture*, 52. See Judd, *Common Lands*, 91.
17. Judd, *Common Lands*, 129.

tently market local rural properties to city dwellers as vacation "homes." This kind of land speculation, a key factor in over-inflated land values and tax assessments, empties out rural communities of full-time residents who alone have the power to create strong local networks of reciprocity upon which stable economy is founded. It was especially these outside, commercial pressures, driven as they were by the profitability of distant markets, that obliged local communities to seek recourse on state and federal levels. Land stripped of stable, full-time, small landowners is prone to mistreatment and waste.

I advocate throughout this essay for strong, united, and uniting governmental leadership in conservation efforts. This is indispensable in a time of nationalized and globalized industry. If we put up with big business, we have to put up with big government—the latter to check the former, not to serve it. It is more to the point of this work, however, to forward the recognition that the moral capacity of the average American for a real appreciation of putting conservation to work in the field will not enlarge unless the average American knows what it means to directly rely on and participate in the local land community. No matter how erudite or sincere, it is a false environmentalism that emerges from a life lived in total dependence on the industrial complex and the engineered environment. As counter-intuitive as this may sound to some, putting people back on the land in a responsibly productive, mutually dependent relationship with it and with one another is likely the best way to advance the conservationist cause.

Related to this disjuncture between land users and those who may see themselves as defenders of the land but who have no real, abiding relationship with it, there is the phenomenon of certain "green" economic models that environmentalists often propose in order to replace more destructive ones in rural areas. The commercial paradigms often forwarded can tend to alienate the public because they appear unrealistic and unsatisfying to the average working person, whose needs, dependencies, and values the far-off environmentalist does not understand. Proposals that forward so-called "eco-tourism" and the arts to revive struggling rural towns come to mind. In my opinion, these are not viable economic engines, especially in rural areas. World travel is not only never eco-friendly, unless one is walking or riding a bike, but these activities are also utterly dependent on the expendable wealth of the privileged, wealth often generated by the very forces that destroy the land. Further still, these activities sincerely strike a struggling rural person as being superfluous at best and downright wasteful at worst, and so morally objectionable. Galleries full of trinkets, often poorly executed, cannot replace the true arts necessary to make a home; to be a spouse; to husband the land; to nourish the commonweal with skill, virtue, and grace; and to bring one's soul into harmony with heaven and earth. Industrialism destroys art as it replaces skill with mechanization, beauty with efficiency, and ability with ambition. In all candor, and more to the point, rural communities have better things to be than mere playgrounds for wealthy urbanites.

Another solution that I often hear forwarded appears to me to embed rural people further in the problem: jobs in so-called green industries and technologies. This, or the so-called environmentalists propose to transform rural landscapes into industrial ones with the proliferation of solar and wind farms, so that yet another rural resource can be extracted for urban and suburban users who clearly use way too much. Conservationists need to be more considerate of rural life and of authentic, working class economic activity, the kind that puts the common person to work with dignity. In a rural setting, this means putting people to work on the land in a diversified productivity where self-sufficiency is the foundation from which market activity flows. This would necessitate keeping rural lands affordable for rural people, and keeping rural lands in the custody of those committed to full-time rural life and the land that underwrites it. It would also necessitate radical changes in American trade and agricultural policies, which unfortunately garner ardent support from rural people but that are ultimately destructive of rural life, especially of small farms. The American Farm Bureau Federation, a non-government conglomerate of agri-business interests, is a key player in promoting policies that destroy rural life and small farms, favoring as they often do the big farms and big farm owners, many of who do not even live on their own land. The small rural landowner and land user is in the best position—perhaps with expert guidance, certainly with a solid Aldo Leopoldian vision of land health and their own goodwill (because small farmers can still farm destructively)—to identify and implement appropriate conservation efforts in order to reinforce the generational productivity and beauty of his homeland. He also has the best hope for gaining a modicum of liberty from the forces that not only undermine his fruitfulness, but also the fruitfulness of the environment. Small rural landowners might begin by organizing their own communities, starting with their own family members and closest neighbors, around the primary goal of local self-sufficiency and economy apart from the juggernaut of global technological/economical hegemony. Rural communities must first take care of and provide for their own from the fat of their land, and invite others to join them in this most dignified and patriotic endeavor—the only endeavor that ensures liberty and freedom.

CONSERVATION

In the late nineteenth century onward, as the Industrial Revolution gained momentum, the question of conservation entered decisively and forcefully into the public discourse of America. The issue was taken up from at least three different angles. First was the concern about the rapid decline of vital resources and the specter of exhausting them entirely. Timber was especially a top concern. From this perspective, conservation's chief aim was the measured and responsible—we might now say "sustainable"[18]—extraction of resources. It took into account human need for the resources of nature and the prosperity we enjoy through them, but sought to bring some equilibrium and mutuality to the relationship. Science also became a large part of the program, dictating from its empirical findings proper methods and approaches to forestry, grazing, water usage, or the utilization of fisheries, for some examples. In modern times, John Evelyn's work *Sylva* can be cited as an early specimen of this kind of approach. Some consider *Sylva* to be one of the most highly influential books on forestry ever published. Originally presented as a paper to the Royal Society in 1662 and published as a two-volume book two years later, *Sylva* addressed the diminished timber resources in England, advocating for the measured management of forest resources to allow for regrowth and regeneration, and the securing of future usage and enjoyment.[19] But even in 1662, *Sylva*'s message was nothing novel. We know that at least one other book on the subject preceded Evelyn's in Europe by over a hundred years.[20]

An approach such as we have just described is what some might limit the term "conservation" to entail. It deals mainly with the question of practicing a more benign use of resources rather than a complete letting alone of the land. Such an approach is disfavored among some environmentalists today. Since Roosevelt's time, we have come to appreciate the complexity of

---

18. For a good discussion on the inadequacy of this word to define conservation and environmental goals, see Freyfogle, *Why Conservation is Failing*, 113–43.

19. Evelyn, *Sylva*.

20. Master Fitzherbert, *Boke of Husbandrie*, published in 1534.

ecosystems. One cannot favor and maximize yields of one species without degrading the whole. It is a downward spiral. If this is the case for sustaining yields of one species or resource, it is much more the case when attempting to sustain yields of two or more resources in the same vicinity. It cannot be done because nature does not in fact work that way; natural resources exist within a complex system of relationships. To work from a more sophisticated understanding of these relationships is what sets environmentalism apart from conservation in the minds of many, though the terms are used interchangeably throughout this work.

Another concern that sets the two terms apart in some minds is the goal of protecting virgin landscapes from any kind of human use. Conservation, insofar as it focuses on human use of land resources, is not enough; we need to let the land alone to do its thing, which we might believe is done better without us. When taken to an extreme, such an approach tends to artificially remove the human being from nature and its processes, which is ironically one of the symptoms of our disaffection from nature, a disaffection that leads to nature's ultimate disfigurement. Still, the idea of virgin landscapes takes an important place within the range of potential and proper land uses that conservation-minded communities must consider, especially because of its benefits, not only on human communities and the human soul, but on contingent lands where resources are being utilized. This second aspect of conservation—the idea of the untouched wilderness—became integral to the conservationist vision early on in America, in the nineteenth century. It is the second angle from which conservationists approached the problem of land and resource protection.

WILDERNESS

The large tracts of "untouched" wilderness encountered by the first European explorers in the New World, and again by the early Western settlers, became an integral facet of the American imagination, but more in hindsight than in foresight. When the frontier disappeared, when there were no more unexplored territories to expand into and no possibilities to pick up stakes and try one's luck further west, a subtle anxiety stirred deep in the American soul. This, coupled with the rise of the ugly, dirty, cramped industrial city, served to transfigure what once may have been considered vast wastelands into a "wilderness"—untouched, unbridled nature as original as paradise itself. What would be the fate of these unscathed tracts of land? Would they be set aside as places of refuge? Would they be protected for future generations so that our posterity can have the same experience of virgin nature that aroused the imaginations, and the appetites, of our ancestors?

There is also a direct correspondence between wilderness lands and lands used for production. For example, wilderness parcels surrounding farmland contribute to the health and productivity of that land. A few of these potential benefits include the provision of buffer zones to slow water runoff, and the provision of habitat for a variety of species, many of which are helpful to the farming endeavor in that they prey on common crop pests. Wilderness areas surrounding farmland also provide erosion control by slowing the movement of wind and water through the landscape, and they contribute to the overall fertility of the soil by gifting their own fertility to the lands that border them, along with clean water. These considerations inspire our efforts to preserve land as wilderness.

POLLUTION AND THE URBAN ENVIRONMENT

The problem of pollution was another factor contributing to the urgency of conservation in nineteenth-century America. As people moved from the agriculturally-based economies of the countryside into the rapidly growing and industrialized cities, the health threats posed by pollution ignited efforts to improve the urban environment. The urbanization of America, a trend that continues to this day (checked only by the troubling expansion of suburban sprawl), has had a devastating effect on the American imagination. One such effect is an increasing disaffection from the land and an attendant disdain for rural life. Counterintuitively at first glance, a recent study has also shown that urban population growth is associated with forest loss, while rural population growth is not.[21] This study took place in many third-world countries that are experiencing similar population shifts as were seen in America during the Industrial Revolution. According to the United States Census Bureau, 7.2 percent of the American population was urban in 1820. By 1930 that number had grown to 56.2 percent, and by 1950 to 64 percent.[22] Currently 80.7 percent of the American population is urban. Between 2000 and 2010, urban population growth continued to

---

21. DeFries et al., "Deforestation," abstract.
22. Gibson, *American Demographic History*, fig. 2-2.

outpace overall population growth by 2.4 percent.[23] In 2008, the world's population was evenly split between urban and rural populations, and the scale has tipped since then in favor of urban dwellers.[24]

This means, of course, that more than 80 percent of Americans and more than half of the world's population do not have regular contact with the land and are not subject to the limitations and conditions of nature. Such people's lives are governed, shaped, and sustained by technology and the engineered human environment rather than by intimacy with the land and by a genuine relationship with the land for survival and prosperity. I used to run a program for youth in my small Catskill Mountain town. I remember one day having some children from New York City in the program, whose parents were quite trendy and clued-up on environmentalism and nature education. When we went to pick some apples from a tree in town, one of the city kids protested, "You can't eat that!" I exclaimed, "It's an apple!" The child refused to take a bite, unable to recognize an apple apart from the supermarket shelves, though she certainly could explain to me the ins and outs of a smartphone and might even have had some knowledge of ecosystems and why we should protect them. No matter what information you give to such people, no matter what kinds of environmental lessons you offer them in school, their value systems will necessarily be affected by virtue of the fact that their daily experience is one of disaffection from nature. Even if such people pay visits to rural and wilderness areas, or believe in doing the right thing for the environment, the only right things they will be left to do will mostly be "green" consumerism and various forms of activism. Such actions are the only actions left to people who do not have a genuine, day-in-and-day-out connection to the land itself, and who do not ever confront the real limitations of nature and of rural experience in general. The experience of most of the world's population is one of disaffection from nature, and this trend is only getting worse. Disaffection from nature, no matter how trendy, hip, and environmental we try to be, only leads to the disfiguration of nature. One such disfigurement is to try to artificially remove the human community from the land in the name of environmentalism.

In the urban, industrial setting, the environmental movement also became aware that it was fighting a class struggle. The wealthy could afford to build their homes away from the polluted, noisy, fetid downtowns. The

---

23. United States Census Bureau, "Measuring America."
24. "Human Population," sec. "Urbanization."

poor could not. It was the poor who were affected most by environmental degradation. To this day, many environmentalists view themselves as liberators of the underclasses.

AGRICULTURE, THE RURAL ENVIRONMENT, AND THE DIVIDED AMERICAN CONSCIENCE

Post World War II America brought a number of new problems to the table. From the twenties through the forties, various land-use disasters such as the Dust Bowl proved to be severe pedagogues for the American public. A heightened sense of the complexity and interrelatedness of the land was growing among conservationists, along with a deepened appreciation for the limits of science to understand and manipulate these relationships.[25] Out of this grew a more ecologically based perspective of conservation, as opposed to one that merely sought to maximize yields of various resources. At the same time, however, agriculture was rapidly undergoing considerable change with the advent of chemical pesticides and industrialized farming techniques. This has had the tendency to industrialize as well as defile the rural landscape, along with the already industrialized cityscapes.

To be sure, the industrialization of farming was in part being driven by necessity, as it still is. As people moved to the cities to enter the job market, rural areas emptied out. Fewer farmers needed to produce more food for a growing urban population who could not produce but only consume. Nonetheless, the economy boomed, and newly affluent Americans, now generally based in urban and suburban locales, grew nostalgic for the countryside and went to nature to play. They became increasingly aware of environmental degradation, and perhaps even began to link it with the affluence they were enjoying, thus finding themselves in a tension between their comforts and their consciences. This was, of course, nothing new, but the scale was unprecedented. Never before had more Americans enjoyed the leisure and the material security that they were enjoying. Such leisure and security, at the same time, allowed for a considered reflection on issues concerning the environment. It is no coincidence, therefore, that in this time of widespread prosperity among a strong and dominant middle class, ecological ideas began to be popularized. The children of the sixties are, by and large, the children of these tensions, which include:

25. For a more detailed discussion of these developments, see Freygol, *Why Conservation is Failing*, 124–143.

- The tension arising from our desires surrounding our lifestyles and standards of living on the one hand, and the knowledge that these cherished lifestyles and conveniences have a very dark side on the other;
- The tension between the opulence and education that affords us the leisure to reflect on environmental issues, even as we wholeheartedly participate in the demise of the environment by our very opulence and leisure;
- The changed relationship with the land itself, from one of dependency, participation, and surrender to its imposed limitations to one of romantic enjoyment, yielding a highly misguided conception of nature and the land as well as an underlying and unexplored disdain for the land's constraints and its affronts to our hard won but illusory autonomy from it.

Such tensions continue to wreak havoc within the environmental movement as well as in society at large. It is telling that the popularity of environmentalism, the appearance on the stage of everyday life of environmental rhetoric, has increased along the same curve that overall wealth, privilege, and urbanization—derived, at least in part, from environmental maltreatment—has increased. Who are the environmentalists? To many a blue-collar worker and rural American the answer seems clear: the environmentalists are the wealthy, the privileged, the urbanite, and the urbane. This perception, though perhaps too often spot-on because the project of conservation has been surrendered to the liberal, is a problem. The cause of conservation belongs to all. It is as American as apple pie. Hunters, fishermen, trappers, farmers, loggers, religious conservatives—all have skin in the game; all benefit when the general citizenry cares for and is connected to the common land. Unfortunately, many environmentalists today multiply their real enemies by fighting imaginary ones.

REVOLUTIONARY STRUGGLE OR COMMON CAUSE?

In the earlier history of conservation, at least as it developed in New England, local relationships of reciprocity upheld by a strong sense of the commons and human dependence on the health of its resources helped communities to self-regulate. The resiliency of the New England landscape, unlike the arid landscapes of the west, was a boon in that it was so quickly forgiving of immoderations, allowing for corrections of use and second starts. As the commercial activity widened, pressures from outside speculators and the distribution of resources to distant markets necessitated checks and balances on state and federal levels because threats to stable, productive, responsible land use moved beyond the reach of the local community. The goal, however, remained largely the same: to ensure the integrity of the commons and equality of access to its bounties and beauties, not only presently, but over generations. As conservation efforts became more top-down, especially under the Progressive-era program, certain disconnects developed between small land users, government bureaucracies, professional conservationists, and urban and suburban elites who championed the cause. One of the unfortunate results in these disconnects was to put the small landowner and petty resource user in a defensive position against distant influences, the very reason these same people sought recourse on state and federal levels in the first place.

Despite these tensions, in a world where commerce is nationalized and globalized on an unprecedented scale, it is clear that strong state and federal leadership is necessary in order to protect the small, stable land user and the resources common to us all. Federal and state leadership in conservation puts the issue where it belongs, in the lap of all the people. Clarity of leadership on these levels can go a long way in uniting disparate social groups and social classes in a common cause that is articulated in terms of public duty as opposed to revolutionary struggle. Indeed, the conservation movement that came to flower under Theodore Roosevelt was undertaken not only without a rhetoric of social conflict—one social group pitted against the perceived or actual injustices of another—but was rather undertaken in the spirit of patriotism. It called forth patriotic sentiments that would supersede internal conflicts and social differences. Roosevelt, in fact, abhorred revolutionary sentiment, identifying it as one of the greatest enemies of the American endeavor, a malevolent spirit that would eventually devastate the nation through internal discord.[26] Competing interest groups without a vigorous national purpose would only leave America divided and aimless, confused and so ineffectual, susceptible to disaster. Such fears are becoming realities in our own time, for our moral imaginations can envision little else beyond the amplification of individual predilections, while our politics are focused on partisanship and special interests, many of which are tangential at best to the real challenges that we

---

26. Hays, *Gospel of Efficiency*, 266–71.

face as a nation. We might take a lesson from Roosevelt, who was a realist about human nature. Whichever special interest group becomes dominant, so he believed, that group would exercise power just as selfishly as the ones they themselves have fought against. History has largely proven the theory.

Roosevelt envisioned a nation of individuals bound together by personal relationships. One's upstanding personal conduct in all one's doings was, therefore, essential to a strong nation. Each individual is endowed with a peculiar moral responsibility. Group-think and internal power struggles were discouraged, even while strong governmental leadership was encouraged in order to unite people in a common cause that transcended petty special interests. While the urban centers tended to breed discontent and social discord, Roosevelt recognized that the real strength of America lay in the rural, agrarian life. It was this recognition that caused him deep concern when confronted with the great population shifts from rural lands to the industrialized urban centers, though he knew that such forces were here to stay. In fact, in December 1908 he appealed to his successor, President-elect Taft, to implement a plan for the improvement and support of country life.[27] America desperately needs such a concerted plan today.

The conservation movement as we have received it at present is severely fractured. The complexity and depth of the problems highlighted in this chapter have only grown worse, and the collusion of government with big business and the globalization of markets does not help the situation. The small landowner has been overpowered, and few state and federal protections guard against his disappearance altogether. Conservation efforts generally reflect the desires and needs of local communities and groups who, through activism and various political channels, strive to realize public policy.[28] As such, these endeavors are often disjointed, lacking the power to gain effective national and non-partisan support, are themselves wasteful of resources, and are implemented haphazardly without clear objectives. Even on state and federal levels, fragmentation undermines unity of purpose. By the time the great conservationist Aldo Leopold reached the zenith of his career in the 1940s, he could complain that conservation was a "house divided" with conservationists working at divergent purposes. Leopold tells the story of a Civilian Conservation Corps member cutting down a dead tree that bore one of the few remaining eagle's nests "in the name of

---

27. Hays, *Gospel of Efficiency*, 270.
28. See Gottlieb, *Forcing the Spring*, 58–59.

'timber stand improvement.' To be sure," Leopold ironically continues, "the tree was dead, and according to the rules, constituted a fire risk."[29]

Today, Freyfogle suggests that such division is evident in "the strand of the movement that has flourished the most of late: tract-by-tract preservation work performed by the Nature Conservancy, the Trust for Public Land, and hundreds of local land trusts."[30] Freyfogle argues that such an approach competes for dollars and support from other efforts, weakens an emphasis on ecological interdependence by a focus on specific parcels, and can serve to cloud the movement's cultural criticisms of free-market capitalism and excessive individualism. He gives an example of the latter:

> When one element of the conservation cause pays landowners to conserve . . . how can another element contend that good land use ought to be a minimum obligation of citizen-owners, enforceable by legal sticks rather than financial carrots? In the flush of successfully protecting the individual parcel, it has become too easy to forget about the larger landscape, about the plight of taxpayers, and about the unceasing, econo-techno-juggernaut that land-trust work often diverts but never really slows.[31]

Finally, Freyfogle concludes his remarks by noting that, "In the name of liberal inclusiveness, many conservation groups now honor a multiplicity of voices. But multiple voices should be the input, not the public output. When conservation speaks with multiple voices, the results inevitably are fragmentation, public confusion, and a compromised ability to deflect critics."[32]

Many people today view conservation as anti-social. Its opponents blame it for hindering productivity, for being a wrong use of government to interfere with private life, and they disparage it as a movement that grabs good, usable land and renders that land useless to the human community. Though it cannot be denied that, at certain points, these kinds of elements must comprise a portion of the conservation effort, history and the public record tell a more nuanced story, and so must environmentalists. For example, when pollution interferes with private life, do not environmental laws help to safeguard that life? Environmental laws protect property owners,

---

29. Leopold, "Threatened Species," 231. Quoted in Freyfogle, *Why Conservation is Failing*, 20.

30. Freyfogle, *Why Conservation is Failing*, 5.

31. Freyfogle, *Why Conservation is Failing*, 5–6.

32. Freyfogle, *Why Conservation is Failing*, 7.

even as they impose limitations. When good land is turned to waste by ill use, does this not stymie productivity and render that land useless to the human community? Conservation efforts may indeed deter very profitable business for a few, but the facts tell us that conservation, in the long run, makes for better business for many, especially when measured over longer periods of time.[33] Conservation and healthy lands spread productivity to more people and into posterity. This is likely dissatisfying news for the few who would profit now, but is nonetheless a compelling reason for many to embrace it. To ask such a sacrifice of one for the sake of many, however, is just hypocrisy if we are not willing to accept limits in other spheres of life for the good and prosperity of the whole.

Perhaps one of the most crippling ailments that the current environmental movement suffers with is moral fragmentation and confusion. Conflicting ethical frameworks serve to render environmental rhetoric incomprehensible. In the wake of the social reforms that came to a head in the Civil Rights Movement of the 1960s, the environmental cause became wedded to many of the ideals and objectives therein advanced. For much good but also for ill, conservation became "environmental justice." As such, its language adopted a rhetoric of liberation and oppression and of personal civil rights, an obscuration of its common objectives and common bearing on all groups. In addition, since that time, the environmental cause has been associated with 1960s counterculture, an association it has not yet managed to throw off, if it has even tried. The association links it with that movement's maverick morality and self-indulgences. It comes across as a social movement, something radical and revolutionary, and is therefore ditheringly received and often viewed with suspicion, serving as often as not to divide people rather than to unite them in common purposes. Accompanying this, it has taken on a decisively urban, cosmopolitan flavor, while also advancing by way of political association preoccupations such as abortion, the LGBTQ agendas, and other such special interests whose objectives remain distasteful to many decent Americans. Unfortunately, the rhetoric and underlying moral visions that bolster preoccupations such as these is too often discordant when considered alongside both the

---

33. Freyfogle cites a 2002 study prepared by the Office of Management and Budget entitled "Draft Report to Congress on the Costs and Benefits of Federal Regulations." It reports that the total aggregated annual costs associated with all major federal environmental regulations had a range with a midpoint of $163 billion, while the range for the total annual benefits had a mid-point of $950 billion (Freyfogle, *Why Conservaton is Failing*, 138n).

conditions of nature and the moral and ethical claims that a strong environmental ethos must endorse. It is this moral confusion and fragmentation that I am most interested in exploring in the chapters to come.

As we have seen in its early roots, at least in New England, conservation grows out of stable, communal structures rooted in tradition and on the land. Conservation, therefore, is about safeguarding the resources that make for life, perhaps especially life in common, including the resources inherent in social institutions and cultural traditions. Conservation is about planning and organization, common purpose, and restraining individual and private interests in a consideration of a common good and a common dignity. Conservation is about maintaining integrity—that of the land and that of our own selves. It is about equilibrium—balancing our desires and ambitions with the realities of nature, of the land, and of the communities that it supports. Conservation is about stability. It is a partnership with place—its history, its present condition, and its potential futures. Conservation is about community—a communion with the dead, the living, those yet unborn, and with the land itself. Conservation, in short, is inherently conservative and deeply moral.

A strong sense and practice of personal sacrifice must be articulated and demonstrated across the entire range of public life if conservationists desire to communicate a clear message and to change culture. The real enemy of conservation is ideological, and conservation's current liberal champions are themselves steeped in the ideologies that make for ruin every bit as much as their opponents are. These concerns and the history of environmental conservancy, therefore, require us to step back for a moment from the war we think we are fighting, and to reflect more deeply about conservation itself. Chiefly, we must reflect more substantially on the moral and ethical fibers that weave together to create a fitting carpet on which can stand a robust and palatable appeal for conservation. If we were to take the issue of conservation more seriously in moral and ethical terms, and to take its history more seriously, might conservation have a drastically different public face and reception than it has now?

Chapter 2

Wrongheaded About Rights

Environmental degradation is a symptom of a flawed culture . . . To halt that degradation, conservationists need to confront these underlying cultural flaws. In the case of the United States, ironically, they take the form of excesses of virtue. They take the form, that is, of cultural beliefs and practices that honor the individual human and individual rights but do so in ways that threaten the well-being of the collective whole.[1]

—Eric T. Freyfogle

Whenever there are in any country uncultivated lands and unemployed poor, it is clear that the laws of property have been so far extended as to violate natural right. The earth is given as a common stock for man to labor and live on. The small landowners are the most precious part of a state.[2]

—Thomas Jefferson

Sometimes the most important question to answer is not necessarily the question you are asking. Conversations between spouses and neighbors, and debates within communities and nations, tend to become gridlocked when the questions that are being debated are ill-formed, unclear, or based in impossibilities. When our concept of an issue—or what is at

---

1. Freyfogle, *Why Conservation is Failing*, 17.
2. Jefferson, "Thomas Jefferson to James Madison."

stake in one—is defective or not well-thought-out, what tends to happen is that people begin to speak past one another. For all the effort they put into the mounting fight, frustration on every side is the only fruit it bears. I fear that our public debates (if we can call them that, as they more often take on the character of a second-grade name-slinging) have reached such a point. National debates are complex, but one of the keys to unlocking some of the current gridlock and relieving some of the frustration is to be found in the ways we conceive of and talk about rights; if, that is, we are willing to think of ourselves less as heroes, liberators, and isolated selves and more in the quotidian categories of husbandmen, handmaidens, stewards, neighbors, and the like.

PROPERTY RIGHTS ARE PROTOTYPICAL

In the realm of rights, property rights are prototypical.[3] Through the nineteenth century, our country produced a well-developed and extensive body of constitutional law dealing with property rights, and almost nothing on freedom of speech and religion, for two examples. Theories of rights began with theories of property rights. Since this is so, since the right to private property is the prototypical right, and since it is also the central focus of most land-use and conservation debates, it would behoove us to spend a little time to study the history of this right in both the ideological realm and in the hard application of the courtroom. A brief look at property rights will help to demonstrate how our understanding of this basic right has tapered over the decades. This is important for two reasons. First, it helps us gain a more nuanced and considerably broadened appreciation of land ownership and its history here in the United States. Doing so will help us to better conceive of a harmony between what we now tend to treat as two irreconcilable extremes, the enigma of private ownership and common interests. Perceiving that such a harmony is indeed possible will allow us to avoid the extremes of an unworkable individualism on the one hand, or a pie-in-the-sky socialism on the other. A strong sense of private ownership coupled with an equally strong sense of public stewardship will make for a more palatable and honorable conservationism in the end.

Secondly, and most importantly for our purposes in this chapter, we take the time for this survey so that we might recognize how our

3. For a more robust treatment of the legal and moral implications inherent in the right to property, see Freyfogle, *Agrarianism*, 83–106.

understanding of rights in general has similarly tapered along the lines of our thinking about the right to property. This tapering of thought is one of the reasons why our public imagination is in irons. Freyfogle points out that many defenders of property rights commonly assert that "landowners possess inherent rights to use their lands intensively, free of restraint, so long as they avoid visibly harming anyone else."[4] We too often hear people following this same line of reasoning when it comes to rhetoric about other perceived rights, such as a person's "right to choose" regarding abortion and sexual behavior. As Freyfogle exhaustively demonstrates from a study of law and history, it is precisely this kind of thinking that is inherently flawed. Freyfogle shows that "Such claims . . . rest upon a poor understanding of how the law has defined landowner rights over the course of America's history." These claims, he continues, "also reflect muddled thinking about how the rights of one owner are restrained by the rights of neighbors and about how private rights fit with pursuit of the public's well-being. Private property is made possible by law, police and courts: it is a social institution in which public and private are necessarily joined."[5] The tendency to want to privatize affairs that are inherently social and communal creates a pernicious, unconstructive, and (in the end) downright fictional basis for general public debate, not only on conservation, but on issues such as marriage, guns, abortion, immigration, speech, religion, and moral conduct.

Acknowledging and caring for a common good is not socialism, as many right-wing thinkers might label it when they are defending a laissez-faire approach to property, trade, and gun rights, for example. Nor is it some kind of high and mighty moral censorship or tedious traditionalism, as liberals might label it when they are defending a laissez-faire approach to abortion, sex, or an attempt at redefining legal marriage, the basic building block of stable societies. Indeed, Freyfogle asks an important question about the role of stability in conservation. Speaking of the "tension within property law between one landowner's desire to develop land intensively and the desires of neighbors and community members to remain free of annoying if not damaging disturbances," he asks pointedly, "When development would undercut the settled life, which interest should law favor? Should the law favor those who want stability and calm, or should it favor instead the more restless owners who yearn to build and reshape?"[6] This is

---

4. Freyfogle, *Land We Share*, 2
5. Freyfogle, *Land We Share*, 2.
6. Freyfogle, *Land We Share*, 7–8.

an important question to ask not only for conservation. We do well to ask such questions when it comes to the proliferation and use of technologies. We do well to ask these questions in the face of globalism, in the realms of art and culture, and when shaping the policies and codes of institutions and communities. We must ask these questions when it comes to weighing the merit of various social changes that are too often forwarded by the perennially discontented, who are always making themselves out to be the saviors and the enlightened ones of the age, and who foist external agendas upon society in a dizzying din of activism and emotional manipulation. Without stability, without calm, without enduring convention, families, communities, and societies crumble. Rights and choices can never belong solely and absolutely to a single person; they are always social. If I had the sole right to do as I please on the property that I owned, how would my neighbors have any right to the uses and enjoyments of the property that they own? Rights are tempered by rights, otherwise they are wrong. Individuals are not their own sole arbiters. To put it positively, rights and choices are reciprocal; we hold them in common.

THE DISFIGURATION OF RIGHTS

With the exception of some places in the South, where large-scale commercial operations—dependent first on indentured and then on slave labor—became the norm, early North American settlers tended to arrange themselves in towns and villages. This arrangement fostered a strong sense of social order and mutual obligation, and it promoted a shared husbandry of the surrounding lands, much of which was open to common use. For an example, as early as 1641, the Massachusetts Bay Colony granted public access to all bodies of water of ten acres in size or greater. Known as the Great Pond Ordinance, it assured citizens the right to fish, fowl, or hunt on these properties regardless of who owned them.[7] For the early New Englander, private ownership did indeed mean an exclusive right to use, but he generally applied this right to homes, yards, gardens, tilled fields, working woodlots, and fenced pastures. Unworked or unenclosed lands, even if a private owner had title to them, were shared by foragers, hunters, fishermen, and others who sought to meet the needs of daily life from the fat thereof.[8] Local communities were not in the least afraid to protect their

7. Judd, *Common Lands*, 7.
8. Freyfogle, *Land We Share*, 23.

interests from outside speculation or unwelcome influences, either. Several towns in Massachusetts, for an example, disallowed the sale of land "to outsiders without the town's permission."[9]

Despite the plantations, the story read much the same in the rural South. Freyfogle cites an 1860 State of Georgia ruling in *Macon & Western Railroad Co. v. Lester*. The latter sought damages from the railroad company when his horse was killed by a train. In rebuttal, the railroad claimed that Lester, by letting his horse roam free, was trespassing, and so the railroad should not have to recompense him. The court denied the railroad's declaration, upholding Lester's on the grounds that, if they did not, they would upset the traditional social order, which shared land in common. "Such law as this," the court noted, "would require a revolution in our people's habits of thought and action . . . Our whole people with their present habits, would be converted into a set of trespassers. We do not think that such is the Law."[10]

In keeping with the founding American ideal where liberty was related to a broad segment of the population owning and working their own small holding, colonies such as Virginia and North Carolina sought to discourage and even actively break up large properties. Thomas Jefferson, when drafting Virginia's new constitution in 1776, wanted to ensure that fifty acres of land go to "every person of full age."[11] These states and others, such as New York, were unafraid to limit the amounts of land a single person or entity could acquire. North Carolina, for example, forbade a person to purchase a tract of land over 640 acres, nor was a single person allowed to buy two tracts of land less than two miles apart. Seeking to discourage land hoarders and speculators, these states also imposed taxes on large landholdings.[12] Though it would prove difficult in an expanding population to ensure everyone the title to some land, the underlying moral intention is clear: no persons or institutions should domineer the ownership of land. The economic independence that land ownership promoted would allow citizens to rise above petty self-interest and serve the common good, and this economic independence, as far as it may be possible,

---

9. Freyfogle, *Land We Share*, 51.

10. Macon & Wester Railroad Co. v. Lester, 30 Ga. 911 (1860). Noted in Freyfogle, *Agrarianism*, 95n10.

11. Quoted in Freyfogle, *Land We Share*, 53.

12. Freyfogle, *Land We Share*, 52–55.

should be the lot of all citizens.[13] The right to private property was subject to moral standards: when it harmed or threatened to harm the common good, not only was it at odds with its original intent, but it also called for regulation. Private property, as understood in early America, was an institution founded for the sake of the good of the whole, not for the maximum advantage of isolated, autonomous individuals. Though large public landholdings that allow common access to these lands are congruent with early American intentions, large corporate holdings are certainly not. The seeds of conservation in America would in fact germinate in the soils of conflict between stable, local land users and expansive corporate domination and exploitation of land resources. Conservation is a fully democratic venture, founded on the protection rather than the diminishment of the right to private property.

As the Industrial Revolution gained momentum, farming became less of a subsistence activity and more of a commercial venture for many people. The old-timers and the poorer citizens would still see unenclosed lands as fair game, but a newer generation looked down on such activities, which often disrupted their efforts at maximizing yields. Laws were enacted to protect the interests of the larger operations, such as requiring all landowners to keep livestock under wraps or else pay for any damage that their wandering animals caused. Nevertheless, woodlands remained for a long time a common inheritance, freely accessed for recreation, hunting, and other public uses insofar as it did not disrupt the owner's activities. When these forests began to disappear at an alarming rate at the hands of the timber operations, it was in the interest of the landowners—that is, the stable landowners who derived their living from an extended, generational husbandry of the land—that states enacted regulations to limit the scope of the timber companies and their attendant activities.[14]

The diminishing tradition of holding lands in common, however simply we have presented it, is elucidatory of how property rights work and evolve. It is also illustrative of the social, communal context within which property rights can only be properly understood. After doing a great deal of damage, timber ventures became the brunt of regulation, not in order to arbitrarily restrict their activities, but to protect the property rights of those who were adversely affected by these activities. Generally, those hurt the most were the people who had long-term relationships with the land. The

13. Freyfogle, *Land We Share*, 55.
14. Freyfogle, *Land We Share*, 23–25.

timber companies, at least with the slash-and-burn, cut-and-run modalities that they were generally operating under at the time, had no enduring stakes in the land. They would harvest and move on. It is justifiable that the long-term users of the land, those who would live a stable life by the enduring husbandry of their parcel, would be protected the most, for these are the ones on which stable society is built, not the near-sighted boom and busts so characteristic of the marketplace. In the end, such regulations improved the overall economy, allowing a wider range of people to be productive over generations.

Similar situations have threatened the Northwest in recent times. Long periods of clear-cutting had left hillsides barren, and hence had degraded waterways by erosion, increased flooding events, and left many rural communities economically destitute. The rising trend of automation in lumber production facilities added insult to injury. Environmentalists stepped in, seeking to slow the cutting by appealing to the Endangered Species Act. Rather than facing up to their complicity in creating the situation, and facing the almost insurmountable dragon of automation, anti-environmental groups consisting of industry leaders, grassroots organizations of loggers, mill workers, ranchers, farmers, miners, off-road vehicle users, and property owners found it easier and more convenient to place the blame of their woes on environmental regulations. Misleadingly naming themselves the "wise use" movement, wielding catchy slogans such as "Jobs versus Owls," and by labeling environmental goals "cultural genocide," these groups took a complex issue and minimized it into tidy mottos and misdirected accusations. The irony in battles such as these is that, by fighting the environmental cause, the landowners and laborers in these communities were strengthening the political weight of the industries that would continue to place profits ahead of their long-term local interests.[15] They failed to see (and this might have been in part because of the rhetoric and tactics of the environmentalists themselves) that the long-term stability of their communities and economies is dependent on the long-term health of their land.

Property rights have a more quotidian aspect as well. Stable landowners, even when using their land relatively responsibly, can still get into squabbles. Property rights exist in order to help settle such neighborly disputes. For an example, as a land-owning New Englander, I have the right to till and enclose the land to which I have legal title. However, my neighbors also have legal title to their land. If one of these neighbors grows

---

15. Bowers, *Mindful Conservatism*, 50.

delectable salad greens, and I raise goats who naturally eye my neighbor's greens with salivating mouths and wagging tongues every day, I had better do all that I can to keep my goats restrained. Otherwise, my right to raise goats on my property would impinge on my neighbor's right to raise greens on his. Because my goats are goats, they will eventually escape and eat my neighbor's greens. When they do, my neighbor can sue for damages on the grounds that I am liable for the harm my animals do and/or that I failed to contain them properly. Considering the long history of such disputes and the legal judgments made on them, my neighbor will likely win the case, which would leave me with a choice to make: build stronger fences, or put the goats in the freezer, for I cannot afford to be a constant visitor to the courtroom. I can protest, "You can't tell me what to do on my land; this is a violation of my right to have goats and bad fences!" Traditionally, the law's answer to such a protest is, "Yes, you have a right to own property, but you also have the responsibility to take other people's interests into account when you use it." If my goats eat your greens, property rights are there to protect you, not me, at least not this time.

All this is to say that there is a relationship here between rights and obligations, and this is how the Founding Fathers of this country—and their children right up into the twentieth century—conceived of rights. We create laws to help settle disputes between neighbors, and what I do on my property is to an extent my neighbor's business because my goats might eat his greens. Rights are not free-standing, but exist only within the context of a network of relationships, and relationships necessitate duties. In the end, I am not and cannot ever be the sole judge of whether or not I am using my property in a responsible manner. To be sure, I still have the freedom to do a lot of irresponsible things on my land, and that is likely for the best. If my activities bring tangible injury to others, however, if they cause substantial risk to others without tangible injury, or if they impede another's enjoyment of their own right to property, then common law imposes limitations. What the shapers of America took for granted was the conception and affirmation of individual rights only within a larger framework of considerations, a framework built by moral reflection, the exercise of virtue, and the duties of obligation. According to this model, rights are to limit the potential abuse of governmental power, not to amplify an individual's freedom of choice. This being the case, we have to ask if our conception of rights has changed over the years. If it has, in what way?

Property rights play a large role in dealing with issues of conservation, but contemporary public debates tend to focus more on other rights, and often with very different assumptions about the nature of rights themselves. For example, look at the First Amendment, the right to free speech. Once designed to limit the government's power to silence critics, free speech, like the right to property, still assumed responsibility on the part of the speaker. It limited the government's power to license the press for fear that the government would not grant licenses to critics, but it did not intend to grant license to each speaker to define their own standard of conduct, nor to promulgate opinions that were treasonous or otherwise deemed harmful to society or morally debased.

Legal cases having to do with antiwar protestors during World War I brought the right to free speech into the fore of the public conscience. Many cases went to court that challenged the government's ability to forbid political protest. Such cases heightened during the McCarthy and Vietnam eras. William J. Stuntz, Professor of Law and Horace W. Goldsmith Research Professor at the University of Virginia, to whose article "When Rights are Wrong" I am indebted for this reflection, cites an event that happened in 1977 as an illustrative example of how an understanding of rights has changed. In that year, the American Nazi Party announced its plans to conduct a march and demonstration through Skokie, Illinois, a town with a high percentage of holocaust survivors. He reflects,

> The planned speech in this famous case was evil and sure to cause great pain, but the pain was not of a sort that traditionally gives rise to lawsuits: the common law has always been loath to grant relief for hurt feelings, even when the hurt is quite real. If the Nazis with their uniforms and their flags, conveying their evil message in a place designed to cause as much pain as possible had a right to march in Skokie, then the march was, legally speaking, nobody else's business. Because of the nature of the activity, there is no web of common law obligations to define a standard of moral, responsible behavior. The only possible source of such a standard is direct regulation by the government. The free speech claim, if it wins as it did for the Nazis, preempts that regulation. Here, rights trump obligations. As far as the law is concerned, the Nazis get to define for themselves where the bounds of propriety lie.[16]

---

16. Stuntz, "When Rights are Wrong," para. 2.

As a goat farmer, my right to property means that I am free to be productive on the land to which I hold title. I can care for, improve, and pass that land on to my children, who in turn can pass it on to their children, free of the fear that it may be taken from us. My right to property limits the government and individuals from intervening or seizing my land and my goats. My neighbors, however, because they also have the right to live peaceably and productively on their property, can file suit against me when my goats get into their greens. For the Nazis, the right to free speech meant that they could essentially say "it is none of your business" to all who might complain about their conduct. In this case, a right is viewed as the freedom to choose without regard to relationships and obligations. Understood accordingly, rights maximize my ability to act on preference, to be my own arbiter, irrespective of others. Stuntz reminds us that, in Madison's or Lincoln's day, it would have sounded nonsensical "to suggest that the government is acting oppressively when it forbids some kind of behavior simply because, in the view of a majority of its citizens, the behavior is evil."[17] But in 1977, the Nazis got their way, as have many other voices for good and for ill. From the waving of the so-called Confederate flag[18] to the ostentatious and intentionally provocative displays of "gay pride" parades, we follow in the footsteps of the Nazis in our appeal to the right of free speech, even when that speech is intended to offend. In this case, it is the understanding of rights as some kind of privatized freedom of choice that wins the day. It is this assumption, so incongruent with the thought of earlier Americans, that turns our public debates into an exercise bike; we pedal and pedal and pedal, and we go nowhere. With this understanding of rights, all that is left is warfare, a clash of perceived entitlements, where the loudest yeller, the best emotional manipulator, the most aggressive lobbyer, or the highest bidder wins. Once intended to limit the misuse of governmental power and the impediments posed by neighbors who unduly crossed their bounds, rights have now taken on a different character, some kind of absolute freedom to choose whatever I please in a world that is otherwise morally neutral and where no objective standards are permitted. What shall we gain by

---

17. Stuntz, "When Rights are Wrong," para. 3.

18. What we colloquially call the "Confederate flag" was never the official flag of the Confederacy. Rather, it was the battle flag of General Robert E. Lee. Lee was, like most historical figures, a very complex man. In a letter written to his wife in 1856, he stated, "In this enlightened age, there are few I believe, but what will acknowledge, that slavery as an institution, is a moral & political evil in any Country."

such an understanding of rights but a society of egoists, where all standards spring from the whims of atomized individuals?

Forces on the political Left have promulgated many speech codes, perhaps especially on college campuses, that are viewed as restrictive in the same ways that environmental and conservation laws are viewed as being restrictive. These "politically correct" speech protocols seek to curb speech that is hostile, impertinent, and rude, as well as speech that questions some of the Left's beloved causes, such as affirmative action, abortion, and the claims dear to the LGBTQ constituency. Despite the Left's failure or refusal to concede that some of the speech that it deems harmless or even actively promotes will very likely be received as being hostile and insulting to various other groups of people, the blameworthy aspects of this program have more to do with the latter than with the former goals. The desire to squelch disagreement on politically contentious topics is unhealthy and an abuse of power. The intention of the right to free speech, after all, is to allow such open disagreement. Insofar as we recognize that our speech is social and therefore must be tempered by concerns that extend beyond personal opinion or some discourteous flaunting of quarantined predilection, we are right, however, to reflect on the moral constraints of speech for the sake of a common good. One would think that both the Left and the Right could be infinitely more sympathetic to one another in this regard, as both seem to desire to introduce moral limits on rights run amuck in a rampant individualism. The problem is that they only wish to do so when it forwards their own rampant individualism, and they may not even recognize that they are doing it at all. In the end, both sides seem capable of only articulating an understanding of rights as idiosyncratic prerogatives that maximize quarantined individual choices without regard to external standards.

If we are to move forward, we must unfetter our conception of rights from the narrow contexts of isolated individuals. If we are to form, be true to, and forward an authentic environmental ethic, we must push on every front to move people beyond this tragically wooden and narcissistic way of thinking. But the first task, and the chief task, is to relinquish such thinking ourselves for the love of the land and the goods that affect the majority of us the most. Those who would honor the land, who would be true environmentalists and conservationists, have a lot of personal work to do. Where madness characterizes the age, sanity is hard won.

Stuntz concludes his article by pointing out that,

Two decades ago lots of people talked about welfare policy in terms of rights, as though it was none of our business how recipients of government aid might use it. Now hardly anyone talks that way; the debate is about what a fair society should do for its poor and how to do it in a way that reinforces (not undermines) society's standards. Not too long ago courts and academics talked about divorce in rights terms, as though all that mattered were the short-term preferences of the spouses. Today the focus is at least occasionally on divorce's social consequences, especially its consequences for children. Moral consequences are still outside the conventional debate, but the direction is nevertheless promising. For moralists, people who believe that moral standards ought to be embodied in law and discussed in public policy debates, that is the only direction worth traveling. And rights as they are now conceived have a powerful tendency to get in the way. Indeed, we might do well to abandon talk about "rights" altogether. Say "limits" instead. That puts the emphasis where it belongs: on the need to place bounds on the fallen men and women who exercise political power. Even better, it takes the emphasis away from where it very much does not belong: on our desire to define our own standards, to maximize our range of free choice . . . Our society has had quite enough arguing about the virtues of choice. We could stand a good deal more thinking and arguing about which choices are virtuous, and which ones are not.[19]

IS CONSERVATION LIBERAL?

Modern Western conceptions of rights developed over a long period of time under the influence of the Judeo-Christian appreciation for the unique value of human persons. Our contemporary understanding of rights, however, came into its own in the philosophical and social reflections of the liberal thinkers. Liberal thought developed out of a growing and upwardly moving middle/merchant class. They were people who worked hard, grew their wealth and influence, and provided opportunities for their children that they themselves may not have had, such as education. The possibility for this kind of advancement defines the "American dream," that through hard work and perseverance one might come to be a freeholder and the aristocrat of his own household, enjoying a certain independence on his own land. Today, however, most of us live in such a way that makes the

19. Stuntz, "When Rights are Wrong," para. 4.

lives of the kings and queens of old look impoverished, and I am not just talking about some 1 percent of us. Mobility, information, securities, comforts, conveniences—we live with privilege heaped on privilege. Classically defined, liberalism "is a political and cultural perspective that honors the individual human and seeks to free him or her from unfair restraint."[20] The restraint that liberalism originally wished to throw off was the feudal system; people often found themselves trapped within manifold layers of social orders and status rules.

Few of us today have an awareness of the provenance of liberal ideas and values. We take them for granted. To confuse matters more, today's "conservatives" from at least the Reagan era on are every bit as liberal as today's liberals. Liberals and modern conservatives both share the same underlying assumptions that have come out of the classical liberal thought of modernity, such as that emanating from John Locke, Renee Descartes, Adam Smith, John Stuart Mill, and Herbert Spencer, to name a few of the giants. The ideas of these men were not formulated in a vacuum. Those with whom they were in dialog are the true conservatives whose perspectives are worth considering, especially when our concern is conservation. We have already discussed some of the key ideas of Edmund Burke, regarded as the founder of modern philosophical conservatism, in the introduction. To fill in these lines a little more, conservatism can be characterized by a skepticism for abstract reasoning in politics. It would appeal instead to a lived experience and tradition. When it comes to morality and politics, human experience over generations is the most reliable source of knowledge, an idea that goes back at least as far as Aristotle, but is generally embedded in all traditional cultures. Within existing institutions, there is a practical wisdom that largely escapes theoretical articulation. Instead, this wisdom is passed down generationally through lived relationships. Though reactionary conservatism may cling to tradition as something static and unchanging, this is not the conservative understanding. Tradition, in the conservative mind, is organic. Tradition undergoes a gentle and gradual flux over many generations. However, when change is considered (and all change must be assessed, as it is not all progress), reforms are understood not only in terms of what seems expedient in the moment, but as a "partnership between those who are living, those who are dead, and those who are to be born."[21] A conservative has the disposition to preserve while also

---

20. Freyfogle, *Why Conservation is Failing*, 47.
21. Bowers, *Mindful Conservatism*, 91.

maintaining the ability to improve.[22] Still, reform should seek restoration, not innovation, and must be practically and not theoretically based.

"Human actions," wrote Burke, cannot be praised or blamed "on a simple view of the object, as it stands stripped of every relation, in all the nakedness and solitude of metaphysical abstraction."[23] Circumstances and relationships determine identity and so what is appropriate; one cannot apply abstract ideologies as universal prescriptions for every situation. Conservatism is not dogmatic reaction, which characterizes some contemporary right-wing movements, but instead believes that a community with a hierarchy of authority is the most conducive to human well-being. Like the slow-food movement, which affirms that the preparation and enjoyment of food has social and spiritual benefits beyond the utilitarian act of taking in nutrition, Burke believed in "slow politics."[24] Such politics are restorative and organic in nature rather than ideological, radical, and revolutionary. It respects time-honored institutions, and does not seek to force upon human communities abstract ideologies, sophistries, and cunning calculations. Though the market economy is viewed as the most conducive to prosperity, markets should work within and not erode customs, as well as the binding fibers of moral and legal obligations and traditions. These undergird stable societies, which also form over long periods in relation to place and land. As one commentator has stated, "If you profess to believe in both the unrestrained market and such old . . . touchstones as family, nation and community, you will . . . discover that the former eats away at the foundations of the latter."[25] Further, conservatives understand that a person's identity is not a matter of choice, but is, to a large extent, given. Identity is determined by an unchosen ancestry, biology, place, community, and so on. When we see how much in our lives is unchosen, then we will come to value the privileges of choice in those few places where we can exercise them.

Alas, history belongs to the victors. The liberal lines of thinking have won the day, while authentic conservatism gathers dust, neglected on a shelf, despite the much-needed clarity it could bring to a host of the pressing concerns of our time, and particularly to the conservationist cause. Locke and Descartes both contributed to our modern notion of the individual as a free

---

22. Bowers, *Mindful Conservatism*, 93.
23. Burke, *Writings and Speeches*, 58. Quoted in Hamilton, "Conservatism," para. 15.
24. Hamilton, "Conservatism," para. 66.
25. Harris, "Spare a Thought." Quoted in Hamilton, "Conservatism," para. 44.

thinker apart from the influence of tradition. Locke also provides us with an idea of private property that would prove compelling, especially to colonizers. In his *The Second Treatise of Government*, he writes, "As much land as a man tills, improves, cultivates, and can use the product of, so much is his property. He by his labour does, as it were, enclose it from the common."[26] Added to this is Locke's notion that, in a money-based economy, the more land one enclosed and so owned, the more the society as a whole would benefit. In other words, the wealthier some became, the wealthier all would become. This latter theory has perhaps proven itself to be true, but only to an extent, for we are currently witnessing in America an ever-widening gap between the wealthy and the poor. In any event, what security or peace can anyone enjoy if the game is to get the most for oneself? Locke's idea, in fact, takes for granted a largely agrarian society, and should seem to us rather quaint. What it does not address, and what Locke himself could not foresee, is how such a notion might play out in the industrialized society that we now need to reckon with, where corporate entities, a new oligarchy of sorts, enjoy the rights of persons and act on a global scale outside of the reach of local governmental systems and neighbors.

Along these same lines, Adam Smith, for his part, gave us the underlying assumptions of free market capitalism, including the notion that free markets would self-regulate, as if by an "invisible hand," to ensure that society would benefit as a whole by the individual pursuit of private interests. Minimizing the role of government would allow this to happen. What is lost today is that Smith's understanding of the free market has as its basis the local community; it was not conceived of as a globally applicable absolute. In addition, while today his argument is used as a means of limiting the use of government to regulate corporate behavior, Smith directed his ideas against the system of mercantilism, which is the governmental support of large economic entities at the expense of local enterprises, such as, for an example, governmental subsidies to big agribusiness, so destructive to the small farm.

A proponent of utilitarianism, John Stuart Mill advanced a conception of liberty that has been distilled in our day to the notion of the individual as a free, experimentally oriented individual who is the final arbiter of standards and values. This has become by far one of the most pernicious notions behind our public behavior and the gridlock of public debates. If such a notion is true absolutely, then there is no chance for society at all.

---

26. Quoted in Bowers, *Mindful Conservatism*, 42.

What we fail to remember is that Mill considered despotism "a legitimate mode of government in dealing with barbarians."[27] Both an indication of his underlying assumption of the importance of moral character in directing the use of liberty to its rightful ends, as well as a justification for the colonialism of his native England, statements such as this allow us to appreciate that the ideas of the classical liberal thinkers were nuanced. It would appear that many of these thinkers worked under the assumption, largely taken for granted, that the people worthy of liberty would not make decisions and take actions without the consideration of moral obligations. To do otherwise would be "barbarian," and would justify the control of a despot.

Finally, Herbert Spencer was largely responsible for creating an ideology out of Charles Darwin's observations. While we generally attribute the saying "survival of the fittest" to the latter, Spencer is the one who coined the term. Not only this, but he applied the concept to social and economic theory, as well as to relations between human cultures.[28]

Every one of these notions discussed above is liberal to the core, and not one represents the thought of conservative thinkers. What today masquerades as "conservative" is, therefore, liberal and libertarian. C. A. Bowers lists the underlying assumptions of liberalism as the belief that:

- Change is inherently progressive;
- individual freedom and the pursuit of self-interest are the highest values;
- ideas and values are a matter of individual judgment;
- emancipation from the hold of tradition is the goal of education;
- nature is a resource that can be improved through human use and management; and
- these assumptions are universally correct and should be imposed on the world's cultures as a matter of moral obligation.[29]

These same assumptions undergird so many seemingly opposing social and political agendas. They are used to support laissez-faire economics and abortion, sexual abandon and guns, environmental and

---

27. Mill, "On Liberty," 18–19.
28. This section is largely dependent on Bowers, *Mindful Conservatism*, 42–43.
29. Bowers, *Mindful Conservatism*, 45.

anti-environmental rhetoric. Perhaps the assumptions themselves need to be scrutinized and dethroned as absolutes that can provide answers to any and all ills. Perhaps we need to understand these assumptions in larger contexts of relationship, reciprocity, moral obligation, and conservation—not only conservation of the land, but of traditional and local values, cultures, customs, skills, economies, and histories, all of which give local communities resilience against the unrelenting and degenerating pressures of global consumerism.

It cannot be doubted that these liberal ideas are powerful, especially when understood in their historical contexts. Neither can it be denied that they have brought about much good. Still, we should take them with multiple grains of salt. For example, those of us who think that individual inquiry free of the bounds of tradition is the only way to exercise true liberty must consider that, when thinking in these terms, we are thinking within the tradition of these thinkers. As much as we would like to congratulate ourselves on our originality of thought, these are not our ideas; we have received them through tradition. This is not a bad thing. We may, however, then want to explore other traditions of thinking, and consider what traditions of thinking, in the end, will provide us with the strongest underpinnings for real culture, stable society, and the philosophical meat to confront the issue of the environment. Certainly, if we were to divorce these liberal ideas from their historical and ideological contexts—i.e., if we were to attempt to throw off responsibility to government, to neighbor, to nature, and to the landscapes that we inhabit—it is clear that we should expect little more than bedlam and ruin on every side. Democracy, classic liberalism, demands that we be mature enough to live virtuous, moral lives. The charge required of a king and a queen was a tall but honorable task: to bring order, peace, and prosperity to their realm and to protect it. Democracy assumes that each and every one of us, whether a small landowner or a CEO of a large corporation, would have the decency, the fortitude, the discipline, the virtue, the moral and ethical tool belt, and (most importantly) the maturity to oversee the realms to which our rights give us charge. This expectation, that we can rule ourselves, is at the core of classic liberalism. To rule necessarily includes the task of limiting, and this is exactly the aspect of classic liberalism that has been lost in the liberalism and libertarianism of our day. Today, the individual is just so, a little autocrat of a nation of one without regard to land or neighbor or moral standard. Insofar as this is how we might define being "liberal" today, conservation does not belong to the liberal cause. Does this mean that every moral choice should be legislated and policed by government? Certainly not! Even still, law is rarely if ever amoral, and America's history demonstrates a certain comfort in using law in order to set moral limitations.

In liberalism's classic definition, and certainly in the thought of true conservatives, individual rights can only be conceived of within the framework of moral obligations. The dignity of the individual was to be found in citizenship, in being a responsible member of an ordered society, even though that society would have its flaws and frustrating aspects and would not allow our personal agendas to always take center stage. Such is the nature of any true relationship, including a relationship with the land. True relationship is by necessity limiting of one's own penchants, ambitions, and fantasies. Mountains are mountains, plains are plains, seas are seas—we do not choose this, we live with them as they are. Conservation, like citizenship, is relational. Right now, relationship is failing at its deepest levels. The ability to remain in communion falters in marriages, in families, and in communities. Unless we address and correct this most horrible of infections, how can we expect to be able to have a right relationship with the land? This is a moral problem, and we must be unafraid to take to task those forces that undermine relationship and communion, including those forces that undermine marriage, family, local community and economy, and the peaceable contentment that would concede to the confines of nature with joyful, reverential obedience.

The imperative of conservation has less to do with secreting off parcels of land from the human community in an effort to keep them unsullied and more to do with using land well. If we cannot use our own bodies, our choices and freedoms, and our rights well, how could we expect that we will use land well? Rights and responsibilities go hand in hand. If we are to genuinely care for the land, it is high time that we grow up and shake off the bratty teenage libertarianism to which we have become so enslaved.

WHAT'S AHEAD?

As has already been asserted, and as might be clear by now, this work does not intend to be a critique solely of the Left, though it is our aim to challenge the current popular belief that conservation belongs there. Commendation can be given to both liberals and conservatives for various reasons, but this work is not meant for praise but to question and to propose new alliances for, and a deepened understanding of, the environmental cause and its inherently conservative (in the classical sense of the term) values. Our brief examination of the changed ways in which we conceive of rights and obligations demonstrates that all of us are guilty of mistaken or inadequate ethical conceptions. Therefore, we will not go without a critical look at various neo-conservative (better to call the kettle black and say "libertarian") narratives that will prove a stumbling block for actualizing not only a true conservatism, but an effective and consistent ethic that would bolster strong families, robust economies, coherent communities, and moral responsibility, as well as conservation of the land. These narratives include those surrounding the notions of indeterminate progress, laissez-faire economics, a narrow individualism, and how these commitments shape the scientific endeavor, its resultant technologies, and our uses of them. Indeed, by way of further rounding out our understanding of the liberal agenda of today's "conservatives," we turn to an examination of these notions as they relate to conservation in the next chapter. This will also help prepare us for a critique of the pet agendas of the Left in the two chapters following. Because they are representative and highly debated, we will use abortion and the LGBTQ movements as case studies. These provide provocative and clear examples of some of the pet agendas of the Left that politically accompany the environmental cause. There, we will demonstrate that the narratives that surround these pet agendas are being formulated under the same guiding principles of neo-conservatism, so vehemently anti-environmental in its rhetoric. Can these principals, then, in the absolutist sense we currently conceive of them, ever help to bolster a robust ethic of conservation? Do such narratives support or detract from the environmental cause, especially when they are placed side by side in a single package such as they are in the voting booth? Would serious conservationists do well to distance themselves from them not only as a political move, but also as a deeply personal commitment in keeping with their love for the land?

It is clear that the underlying assumptions about rights, morality, human personhood, and nature on both sides are essentially of the same liberal provenance. Conservation, as it will prove, belongs to no current political camp, but to those who would cherish a true conservatism extended not just to include human society, but also to the land on which all societies depend. To cherish human society and the land is indeed true conservatism. In it lies the kernel of a natural and proper patriotism.

Chapter 3

Husbandmen, Households, and Economies

I am He, you are She;
I am Song, you are Verse,
I am Heaven, you are Earth.
We two shall here together dwell,
becoming parents of children.

—*Atharva Veda*, 14.2.71.

Representing heaven and earth, I have made husband and wife. This is the beginning of the world.

—Tenrikyo, *Mikagura-uta*.

And I saw the holy city, new Jerusalem, coming down out of heaven from God, prepared as a bride adorned for her husband.

—Rev 21:2.

THE SUMMER HAS REACHED its peak, and already the discerning lungs detect the hints of fall in the cool mountain evenings. The days pass one like the other, no day fully in sun, no day fully in rain. Now incandescent, now under the darkening pall of thunderclouds, light and rain in spectacular displays penetrate into the open fields, the forest edges, the opulent mountainsides, wetting and impregnating, causing the fertile earth to bring forth life out of the dead. The sovereign sky full of thunder, scorching sun and soaking rains, granting its gift; the earth at rest and open, receiving the gift of sky, bringing forth and sustaining new life. Without a contest of power, without a thought, or a question, or a notion that anything could be amiss, sky and earth though two, are one. The bustle of nesting is over by now, and the last of the fledglings come of age in fast preparation for the changes to come. A first autumn, a first winter, and then a first go at progeny; the courting, the pairing, the nest-building, the long lingering in all weather to protect the promise of new life, and the brief but taxing forages to feed their own, to give the life that is theirs, so that the giving and the life can endure.

HOUSEHOLD, ECONOMY, ECOLOGY

Since ancient times, people of all cultures have been privy to this enigmatic truth: opposites are coincidental and complimentary, and their interplay is what upholds all life and existence. Most of our ancestors—especially in the quotidian, earthbound activities related to marriage, raising children, and gaining sustenance from the land—understood themselves to be an integral part of this spectacular cosmic waltz. They did not merely appreciate or value it; they participated in it and celebrated it, often unreflectively and so wholly. The intuition presented itself in many forms. For example, the two wedding hymns quoted above conceive of the union of groom and bride as the union of heaven and earth, while the passage from the book of Revelation envisions the union of heaven and earth as that of a marriage. The coming together of husband and wife is not merely an isolated event wrought by personal preference or choice. It is a participation in the miracle and fecundity of the universe. It is the union, the reconciliation, of coinciding opposites, and that union, as when the sun and rain penetrate the fallow soil and bring its seed to life, is a union on which the continuation of life depends. The imagery carries over throughout the world. The Taoists are well known for their appreciation for the life-sustaining interplay of yin and yang, the masculine and feminine principles in nature. Plato, Aristotle, and other classical philosophers reflected profoundly on the relation of heaven and earth, of the One with the many. The book of Genesis in the Old Testament presents to us an image of God as Father of the universe, whose seminal Word goes forth into the unformed earth and makes it fecund and fertile. Hebrew prophetic literature depicts God as the husband of his chosen people, that they may bear life to the world.[1] Such nuptial imagery, as it is called, was advanced by the Christians in the example of Mary, who receives the Holy Spirit, the Spirit of the Father, and is impregnated, bringing forth the Christ child for the salvation of all. Christ himself is hailed as the bridegroom and the church, the New Jerusalem, as his bride. This marriage of heaven and earth, and subsequently the union of differentiated complimentary opposites such as hot and cold, day and night, and self and other, has been a truth that our ancestors in nearly all cultures largely took for granted.

Our own lives on and relationship with the land have been conceived of in similar metaphors. One who worked the land "husbanded" that ground. We have historically conceived of this relationship as a kind of marriage, with all of the implications of marriage. The husbandman put his substance into the earth, making love to it in order to increase its fertility and yield. He did this for his own life, for the life of his family and community, and (if he did it well) for the life of generations yet to come. As when a child settles into his mother's lap, or as a man settles into bed with his beloved at the end of the long day, the earth would finally take him back into her bosom, earth to earth, dust to dust.

Marriage still provides a fruitful conceptual ground on which to base a sound ethic, not only of human relationships, communities, and economies, but also of conservation and care for the land. Marriage emphasizes stability, mutual self-gifting, and life-long commitments, come what may. It demands the renouncement of possibility for the sake of the actual, the limiting of choice for the sake of deep connection, the shunning of the trivial for the sake of true intimacy, and of variation for constancy. The task of marriage is to find fullness, pleasure, and fulfillment in the routine give-and-take of domestic affairs. The serious-minded conservationist and environmentalist cannot do better but to stand on commitments such as these. Conservation requires this manner of heroic love. All of these commitments undermine and challenge the current social and economic forces that inspire neglect, disdain, abuse, and the disfiguration of the land, for the land is constant, imposes limitations, and thrives in routine. Though it is in continual, living flux, the land yet seeks balance and stability instead of the new and the novel; it is inherently conservative, albeit in its own sumptuous, extravagant way.

1. See especially the book of Hosea.

The Disfiguration of Nature

Nowhere is the dynamic conservatism of nature more prominent than in the reproductive process, and in the cultural pedagogy that has traditionally taken place within familial and communal structures. This holds true not only for the human being, but also for most creatures. For countless generations over millennia, animals of all species have migrated along the same routes, returning to the same places to rear their young. When these patterns are disrupted by the destruction or fragmentation of these routes and destinations, their populations generally suffer. The monarch butterfly provides a proverbial example. Dependent on the milkweed plant alone as a carrier for her eggs and generational migration routes for winter survival, the monarch butterfly is struggling due to habitat loss and fragmentation along its range. Our lust for the new and novel, our lust for so-called "progress," is antithetical to the ways of nature. Karl Marx was well aware of the power and tenacity of this natural conservatism as it played out in human families and communities. For this reason, his social and economic theories sought to undermine the role of the family and of communal structures apart from government, such as religious institutions. He recognized that the pedagogy that takes place within these networks presents a robust challenge to the socialist state's near-total claim on people's lives, a claim that is also being asserted by free market capitalism and the corporations who would see us as little more than units of production and consumption. It is a well-known statistic that, in San Francisco, there are some ten thousand more dogs than children, where dog owners routinely spend about $10,000 a year on their "best friend."[2] Marx would certainly have taken note here of the capitalists' achievement in undermining family units for the sake of the pecuniary system.

As the previous chapter does not disparage rights per se but presents a more rounded way of conceiving of them, so this chapter will do the same for capitalism. Capitalism, the system in which production and distribution are carried out by private (as opposed to state) interests, is undeniably the only appropriate basis for economy in a democratic society. It has proven itself by the generation of incredible wealth, clever innovation, and much good. However, we would be lopsided in our thinking if we did not also consider some of the ills that it has fostered. I believe that capitalism works best on local scales, when it is grounded in face-to-face relationships of reciprocity, but does great damage as a global ideology. Another way this might be said is that capitalism, like rights, needs to be understood and

2. May, "S.F.'s Best Friend."

considered in terms of relationship rather than merely as the atomized pursuits of atomized individuals and—inasmuch as they are legally regarded as individuals—faceless corporations. Economy is inherently relational, and it is no coincidence that it shares the same prefix as the word "ecology." "Eco" is from the Greek *oikos* (οἶκος), meaning "household." Again, for both ecology and economy we find the domestic metaphor of household, implying marriage, family, community, place, and the relationships of procreation, production, and exchange that bind them. If economy is the system of relationships and canons governing the proper management of a household, then it is intimate, organic, and local, not impersonal, ideological, and global.

The economic forces of global capitalism are in fact destructive and subversive of family and locally developed cultural systems and economies. Intentionally or otherwise, the unrestrained global market entices people's commitments away from the local, and so away from familial and communal ties, thus leaving the aged alone and isolated, and the children without roots. It would pit distant, faceless peoples against one another, favor efficiency over labor and sustainability, sway our loyalties away from that which we have toward that which we do not have in an adulterous aspiration. It would convince us of the possibility for limitless progress and production, and so limitless pleasure, if only we threw off all prudence; it would beguile us with a glittering cosmopolitanism, a chance to have it all, and all at the expense of a necessarily limiting and sober connectedness to kin, culture, neighbor, and place. It would reduce the mystery of life in an objective world of wonder to a tyranny of the individual ego and of its desires imposed on that world. Divorced from culture and place, such a one finds his or her only purpose in the amplification of autonomous choices and the placating of unchecked desires, most of which have been created by the manipulations of the marketers and the swaggering displays of the exhibitionist elites. Environmental writer and educator C. A. Bowers notes that

> Recently, molecular biologists have identified the dynamics of one of Nature's most conserving processes: that is, how the instructions encoded in our genes, as well as in the genes of other organisms, reproduce over thousands, even millions, of years, species-specific characteristics. While exceptions continually occur, variations are usually minor and, in most species, slow to take hold. This process

of biological reproduction in no way represents the modern way of understanding change as a linear form of progress.[3]

If we desire to approach a true ethic of the land, a true ethic of conservation, and a true love of the earth, the routine metaphors of marriage and reproduction, of tradition and posterity, of households, are not to be disdained as a grounding rod for environmental rhetoric. Indeed, the imperatives and demands of marriage present to us an almost opposite disposition to that formed and forwarded by consumerism, the driving force behind environmental degradation. This chapter will open out these assertions, laying the groundwork especially for the two chapters that follow.

LOCAL DIFFERENTIATION AND GLOBAL MONOCULTURE

An organism would not survive without integrity. By integrity, we here mean the maintenance of a specific form and structure, a differentiation. This maintenance, for complex organisms anyway, is achieved by the immune system. Not just a system of defenses aimed at eradicating certain invaders, the immune system chiefly helps the organism to distinguish itself from what it is not. Were it not for this response, life on this planet might as well be one fused blob. The possibility for self arises from the immune response, which does not come full-blown from birth, but grows in response to certain challenges to the integrity it seeks to maintain. Edwin H. Friedman, in his book *Failure of Nerve: Leadership in the Age of the Quick Fix*, relates an experiment that was conducted in 1970. "Two organisms from the same species that had not developed immune systems were moved closer and closer toward one another. At a certain threshold of proximity, the smaller one began to disintegrate, and within twenty-four hours it had lost all the principles of its organization."[4] The smaller organism was not destroyed by a hostile act on the part of the bigger one; it merely lacked the means to maintain its integrity in the overwhelming presence of this larger organism. When organisms that lack immune systems touch, they simply fuse as one. This had already been known. But the experiment of proximity revealed surprising results, results that have profound bearing on how we

---

3. Bowers, *Mindful Conservatism*, 7.
4. Friedman, *Failure of Nerve*, 180.

think about the integrity, not only of individuals, but of marriages, families, communities, and nations.

The integrity of familial and, by extension, communal relationships, intergenerational in nature and so connecting the past with the future, is necessary in order to keep consumerism and unhealthy dependencies in check. Whereas families and homes were once economic units in terms of production, and were bound together in part because of this mutual imperative, they have now become economic units only in terms of consumption, which blows them apart.[5] Families were once required to work together for their survival and mutual benefit. An individualistic bias, combined with the lure of expanded options and mobility, have undermined these obligations, now viewed as repressive and backward. Family units themselves have thus borne much ill-treatment, not only corporally but also philosophically. Herbert Marcuse's influential 1966 tract *Eros and Civilization* stated it clearly. Believing that the "will to gratification" would overcome "the established reality," Marcuse rails against "the repressive order of procreative sexuality."[6] Such a sentiment reveals an incredible disaffection from, and disregard for, that aspect of nature central to family life, now darkly viewed as a "repressive order." The goal of Marcuse's sexual liberation is manifestly clear: "a disintegration of the institutions in which the private interpersonal relations have been organized, particularly the monogamic and patriarchal family."[7] Such liberation may sound fun, but the worldview surrounding Marcuse's ideas is downright creepy. It represents a cultural iconoclasm, and is inherently anti-civilization. The belief is that ultimate self-absorption and self-interest ("the will to gratification") leads to ultimate liberation. Of interest is this belief's remarkable correspondence to the notions underpinning laissez-faire capitalism and unfettered consumerism, which is the ideology from which it springs, a point to which we will return shortly. Of greatest concern now is its bearing on the environment, for the liberation one is seeking in this program is a liberation from the natural order itself, from biological patterns of procreation and the ties of kinship, ties that form the very backbone of stable societies and human culture. It represents a profound disdain for, and disfiguration of, the limitations of nature, and it seeks, in the end, a liberation not only from external obligation, but also

---

5. "Industrialization—Family," para. 1. See also Smith, "Impacts of the Industrial Revolution," paras. 1–2.

6. Quoted in Kimball, "Some Perils," para. 3.

7. Kimball, "Some Perils," para. 4.

from love. Many similar sentiments would be promulgated in the wake of Marcuse's work, following along the same paths that he took. They would emerge especially from the pens of gay and lesbian writers such as Foucault. There can be no conservation, no love for the earth, if the innate bounds of nature are viewed as sinister and repressive, or if our only gratification in life is found in unfettered narcissism.

Localized networks of reciprocity and self-reliance, including family units, are like organisms. As such, they need healthy immune systems and to be free from pollution. They must be able to protect themselves from toxic, degrading influences. They must have the freedom and the supports to maintain a certain integrity and differentiation. When this differentiation is under attack, they either tend to collapse, give in, or become radicalized in a desperate attempt to keep their integrity, baring their teeth and claws. While many forms of terrorism are related to the fight response, in driving across America one sees the results of the collapse response in countless immune-deficient communities. The traveler approaches every town via a commercial strip. The strip looks the same from coast to coast. Friendly only to the automobile and to efficiency, it rebuffs pedestrian passage and the neighborliness of authentic community and economy. It spurns all beauty. Everywhere we see the same logos, the same businesses, the same products on the same shelves, all of which are funneling wealth to the same people. If we ever find the town center, we generally encounter an emptied-out downtown where the unique local architectures and cultural relics languish in a general state of neglect, as if forgotten.

As far as conservation efforts are concerned, we must respect and encourage the integrity of localized networks insofar as this kind of integrity is a source of inner strength. Such integrity gives communities the willpower to protect themselves from a precarious reliance on distant resources, from life in the shadows of super-sized corporations, and from damaging and inappropriate influences. The libertarian goal of creating an unfettered global monoculture based on consumption and individual autonomy is an attack on this integrity and is destructive to these grassroots networks and local identities. Dependencies on anonymous and faceless players becomes the norm. It introduces the poisonous notion that people would be better off if they were elsewhere, or that our places would be better if they were other places, or that happiness would be fuller if only we had this or that. Worse, it introduces the demeaning ideologies that would paint our lives on the land, our communities and traditions, and the basic and natural processes of procreation and familial subsistence as repressive and sinister, all while comparing these baleful limitations to the bright freedoms of unlimited individual gratification and consumption. The cause of conservation cannot stand side by side with such ideologies, and neither can a true conservative.

Much of economic growth is achieved by the relentless pursuit of automation, which by design factors the human element out of the production process, and so labor and jobs. Skills—for countless centuries an expression of pride and personal mastery—are lost. For example, my wife and I currently live in a beautiful stone and timber building erected in the early 1920s. While at one time masons and timber-framers were common in our area, it is becoming increasingly difficult to find people who have the skills to make repairs on this architectural peach. The one mason we have found to do repairs takes advantage of our need of him by charging exorbitant prices and doing shoddy work. The latter is an argument for a capitalistic system; healthy competition can work to the advantage of the buyer. When, however, global competition and mechanized production have wiped out the local tradesman, where can we turn when we need the trade locally? We are not here disparaging capitalism, but we do disparage the libertarian idea that markets automatically self-regulate. As long as the human condition is prone to greed and short-sightedness, as long as people themselves are unable to self-regulate and accept the limitations that larger considerations than personal profit require, then we cannot expect markets to govern themselves. Markets are, after all, driven by peoples' ambitions and blindness. Too great a faith in human reason and individual autonomy, a liberal agenda if there ever were one, can lead to very unrealistic expectations, denying the need of human governance and for the imposition of moral obligations even in the face of hard evidence. When nationalized and globalized markets impinge on local communities and economies, as they have in our community by replacing the work of masons with easily installed, manufactured faux stone products, then these local systems need to be able to protect themselves against the colonizing influences that threaten them. If we think otherwise, then we disparage the very foundations of democracy.

Should my example of the mason (and, by extension, the quarryman) seem too quaint, let us look at a few more troubling instances of libertarian global market forces undermining a local community's ability to self-govern and self-regulate. The World Trade Organization (WTO), based in Geneva, Switzerland, has a stated purpose of creating a level playing field for global business. Its purpose is to ensure that no corporation will be disadvantaged by national and more localized laws and policies. This requires that the principles of laissez-faire capitalism take precedence over all other political entities, an alarming agenda. Essentially, the WTO, working in conjunction with the World Bank and the International Monetary Fund (IMF), has made governments subject to markets. These forces work to forge, often against the desires of local communities, a global monoculture that is industrial in character and formed by the whims of the market. It does this by adjudicating cases between corporations and governments, and by imposing penalties on countries not in compliance with its rules and free trade principals. For an example, Venezuela made the claim that the US Clean Air Act would force their oil refineries to change their means of production, and so incur costs, in order to sell their product on the American market. The WTO ruled against the United States, and in 1997 the Environmental Protection Agency complied with the ruling and lowered the existing emissions standards, clearing the path for foreign refineries to sell their filthier gas at American pumps. How patriotic of us to comply! When the European Union ramped up food standards and banned meat raised on artificial growth hormones, the US cattle industry took them to task through the WTO. This time America (or, shall we say, American cattlemen) won, effectively denying the European Union the right and the ability to set their own standards for food safety. What a fine show of our commitment to freedom and self-governance! Can we even suggest that we have a free market if we are not free to govern it as we deem appropriate?

In Canada, the fact that 85 percent of all magazines on the newsstands originated in America caused some concern to Canadian business owners. In an attempt to foster its own local periodicals, Canada offered a favorable postage rate to Canadian publications. At the same time, it passed a tax law that gave incentives for Canadian advertisers to buy ads in Canadian publications. The United States brought up charges against Canada through the WTO, claiming that such policies obstruct fair competition. America won, forcing Canada to repeal the laws that it had established with the intent of protecting its own economy and culture. The Trump administration has produced much rhetoric about protecting and fostering local jobs, but practical efforts to do so will be difficult indeed if the WTO continues to reign. That they do continue to reign is more likely the central concern of this administration, though Bill Clinton also shared this agenda.[8]

8. These examples have been cited from Bowers, *Mindful Conservatism*, 31–35.

Cancer has been described as "a renegade system of growth" with the hallmark characteristic of "unchecked growth that progresses towards limitless expansion."[9] The capitalism.org website defines human freedom in frighteningly similar terms:

> To live rationally by one's reason in society, man needs only one thing from his fellow men: freedom. The freedom to live for oneself, neither sacrificing oneself to others, nor sacrificing others to oneself—the freedom to pursue one's own happiness. It is this freedom that unleashes the creative potential of man's mind, resulting in a society of nationwide peace, *continuous progress* and *boundless prosperity*.[10]

Not only should the similarities between cancer and the underlying assumptions of laissez-faire economics trouble us, but we are left to question the rationality of the latter. The rhetoric sounds well and good. On the face of it, who would not desire such a freedom? And yet, these notions seem to be based more in idealism than in reality. What happens when the freedom of one impinges on the freedom of another? We have already explored such questions, and the legal responses to these questions by American courts, in the previous chapter. Such a sentiment as this abuses the notion of freedom. Is the eagle free? Only in her limited sphere. She is free in the air and on the wing, but she is limited on the ground to stumbling and hopping clumsily around. Are the fish of the sea free? Only in the sea. Out of the water, or if their water is poisoned, they are as good as dead. Should I be free of the complaint of the person I have poisoned in my free pursuit of happiness and profit? No one can live without sacrificing others to oneself, nor can anyone live without making sacrifices for the sake of others. We should have the love and the maturity to recognize, accept, and make these sacrifices in our own freedom, as the founders of this country expected we would. When we do not take this path, but instead are unable to self-regulate (as a cancer cell), we must be restrained. It is this immature abuse of freedom, this ideology so wildly disaffected from reality and its demands, that leads to the necessity for regulation. We must admit that a similar immaturity—one that refuses to bear the risks of real life and incessantly blames others when things go awry—is also behind the promulgation of multifarious regulations. These kinds of regulations, and the litigious culture that sustains and promotes them, need also to be curbed.

---

9. "What is Cancer," para. 1.
10. "Why Does the Individual Need Freedom," para 1. Emphasis mine.

Still, it is impossible to live without limitation and sacrifice; all the evidence points to this fact. Are we to suppose that asking loyalty from employees is not asking them to make limitations and sacrifices? Are we to suppose that the mining company that blows an entire mountain away for coal has not asked anything, or anyone, to sacrifice something? The fact is, if you pass gas in a crowded room, others will have to smell it, and if you pollute the water, others will have to drink it. It is time to grow up. Consider these words from the Hungarian financier George Soros:

> Although I have made a fortune in the financial markets, I now fear that untrammeled intensification of laissez-faire capitalism and the spread of market values to all areas of life is endangering our open and democratic society. The main enemy of the open society, I believe, is no longer the communist but the capitalist threat . . . Too much competition and too little cooperation can cause intolerable inequities and instability . . . The doctrine of laissez-faire capitalism holds that the common good is best served by the uninhibited pursuit of self-interest. Unless it is tempered by the recognition of a common interest that ought to take precedence over particular interests, our present system . . . is liable to break down.[11]

Teddy Roosevelt would have agreed wholeheartedly.

Another requirement of consumer culture is that people not become so fond of their devices and gadgets that they hang onto them forever. Constant innovation protects against this, as does planned obsolescence. Each new model needs to find a receptive market, while each old model finds a landfill. The quasi-religious lore of progress undergirds an economic tactic such as this. It is a lore that disparages what is old and of the past for the promise of the new and the novel and the improved-upon. Such a disparagement for the old, such a frenetic focus on the state-of-the-art, is another force that undercuts familial and communal integrity. The industrialization of food, for example, has supplanted traditional knowledge of plants, animals, and the land, as well as the familial and social activities that once surrounded the growth, preparation, and enjoyment of food. Innovations in digital communications perhaps provide a better example, which we currently see supplanting the embodied, face-to-face relationships that give families and communities integrity and structure. To be sure, some traditions need correcting when they base themselves in the worst of human

---

11. Soros, "Capitalist Threat," paras. 1, 12, 13.

nature, either by design or by distortion. But discernment is needed when we throw off the old for the new. When we judge by a broader set of standards, the time-tested often proves the better way.

I have a friend who was required in the early 1960s to take a college course in "leisure time studies." New technological advances, so it was thought, would lead to such massive amounts of wealth for all and little work for anyone to do. Therefore, students had to be educated in how to use this free time wisely. Despite the empty promises, people in industrialized societies currently work considerably more than those in non-industrialized ones, with little time for parenting and participating in those activities that form the groundwork of solid, resilient local communities. The idea of educating people to use time wisely, however, is a good one; if only our educational systems would focus less on innovation for its own sake, or for the sake of making money on novel things, and more on making wise decisions, not only regarding what we do with time, but with technology, liberty, and the land.

An unrestricted globalized economy also gives big employers and the providers of the goods and services we have become so fond of (and dependent on) the opportunity to blackmail communities and governments. If they do not receive the tax breaks and privileges they desire, if they are strapped with environmental regulations, they will pull up stakes and bring their operations elsewhere, where wages are cheap and the regulatory environment is more favorable. We are asked to lower our standards for the candy they offer us, and we too often willingly oblige. This is another way that unchecked market forces diminish the integrity of familial and locally embedded relationships. Capitalism works capitally on localized scales, especially when tempered by the informal, neighborly socialism that once marked the American way of life, but it wreaks havoc as a globalized, absolutist ideology.

LAISSEZ-FAIRE EVERYTHING

We will end this chapter by noting that laissez-faire capitalists, because they are essentially liberal and libertarian, are required by their absolutist notions of individual rights to promote the right to abortion.[12] Because of the Left's commitment both to the environmental cause and to abortion, we will explore this latter issue and the rhetoric that surrounds it presently

12. See, for example, http://capitalism.org/category/abortion/.

in order to determine whether this rhetoric is congruent with the value systems that would bolster the conservationist cause. In keeping with their core commitments, laissez-faire capitalists would likewise tend toward an unhindered use of their sexuality. Free-market guru Ayn Rand promoted some strange and narcissistic views regarding sex, accepted her adulterous relationship as perfectly rational, and often declaimed a disdain for the traditional family.[13] Perhaps the real environmental showdown will be between the true conservatives and the promoters of the libertarian, laissez-faire lifestyle. The true test of allegiance to conservation, to the earth, will be measured not by party affiliation, but instead by a willingness to conform one's own values and actions to those requisite to a sane, stable life lived close to the land. If this sounds boring, I invite you to try to do it. You will soon find yourself in the midst of a sweeping, morally charged mêlée, not only with the culture around you, but with the secret corruptions and desires of your own heart. You will find yourself out on a limb in a real adventure, perhaps for the first time, in an undertaking with great meaning and consequence, one that will test your resiliency and the strength of your integrity. You will bear sacrifices you thought you could never bear, and find sweet redemption in them.

I do not necessarily promote an attempt to turn back the clock to a perceived simpler time. I only insist that we govern how we move into the future and what we choose to destroy for the sake of that future. Renouncing the sham, tragic heroism of rampant and unrealistic individualism and instead learning to think in the quotidian—but all the more heroic—categories of marriage, family, and communal life can go a long way to help us in this task.

---

13. Alexis, "Ayn Rand's Objectivism," para. 25.

Chapter 4

The Moral Logic of Conservation: Abortion and the Earth

Hear the word of the Lord, O people of Israel;
for the Lord has a controversy with the inhabitants of the land.
There is no faithfulness or kindness,
and no knowledge of God in the land;
there is swearing, lying, killing, stealing, and committing adultery;
they break all bounds and murder follows murder.
Therefore the land mourns,
and all who dwell in it languish,
and also the beasts of the field,
and the birds of the air;
and even the fish of the sea are taken away.

—Hos 4:1-3

OVER THE TWENTY YEARS or so that I have been involved in conservation, even if only as a cheerleader, writer or thinker, there has always been something about the movement that rubbed me wrong. In my better, quieter moments, something about what I saw and heard from those around me who shared my concerns for the environment just failed to jive. It has taken a very long time to gain a modicum of clarity about exactly what the sources of this discomfort were. As I have honed in on these sources of discomfort over the years, I have also found myself more and more alienated from the movement itself, much to my chagrin. I value good, healthy land—virgin or otherwise responsibly used—as much as ever, perhaps even more. However, I find that I cannot stand with the majority of environmentalists and affirm what they affirm. I find the ethical milieu among environmentalists to be confused, undisciplined, unnecessarily and unproductively revolutionary, and (quite frankly) downright hypocritical. Perhaps I am just getting older. Still, despite the coagulation that comes with age, and despite the value I put on clarity and soundness of thought, I do not consider myself as a black and white thinker. I understand well the complexity of the human heart and that we are all, in the end, walking paradoxes. That is what makes us living beings and not machines. Yet, as I have come to more deeply appreciate the quality of mind and soul that the land and the love of it requires, I have also come to recognize that the environmental movement is not at home with its many current political and social bedmates. It is not at home among the ranks of radical liberals any more than it is at home with laissez-faire economists. If it remains there, as at least a publically perceived liberal cause, its moral logic will ever be compromised and confused, and its message unheard and unheeded by many Americans. In this chapter, we will briefly examine why I have come to believe that this is so, using abortion (another issue forwarded by the Left) as a case study.

As a movement belonging now almost exclusively to the Left, environmental rhetoric and the policies that it proposes are fired at the American public alongside a dizzying array of other agendas. Some of these agendas are wholesome and good, such as access to decent healthcare for all, while others are quite radical and belong to very specialized interest groups. The track record of such groups shows that they are often inconsiderate of a common good and are, at worst, disdainful of the values that have shaped, and continue to shape, America. The objective of some of these groups is to engineer out of society all that does not or will not affirm their lifestyles. They aim their sites on traditional institutions that serve to cohere societies together, such as family, and pull the trigger. Unfortunately, it is difficult for the American public to disentangle these agendas and deal with them each on their own merits. They would in fact find that, even if they tried, they could not. If I vote for the environment, I am also voting in support of abortion and the LGBTQ agendas, to name but two of these entwined programs. The worst thing of all is that the rhetoric, the tactics, and the purposes of these groups are often wholly inconsistent with the aim of land conservation and its requisite moral attitudes. These attitudes include but are not limited to a deep respect for, and obedience to, the limitations of nature; personal responsibility; sacrifice for the sake of the other; fidelity; stability; and self-regulation.

The political group that claims to care for the environment, that has taken upon itself the environmental cause, is also the political group that bolsters the practice of abortion and the ethical worldviews that surround it, and offers unquestioning support to various LGBTQ interest groups. Environmentalists should bemoan their party's commitment to abortion. If they would loosen their grip on this issue alone, they would likely still be in office, where the environmental cause—infinitely more crucial to the common good than abortion's legality—would continue to advance. Yet, supporters of conservation would do well to not merely give up on abortion for the sake of political compromise. The attitudes that lie behind the practice and proliferation of abortion—attitudes elemental to the founding principles of organizations such as Planned Parenthood—are incongruent with the environmental cause. The same can be said of many of the core assumptions forwarded either explicitly or implicitly in LGBTQ narratives. In the next two chapters, we will explore why the core attitudes, assumptions, aspirations, and ethical commitments that have shaped these movements are almost wholly incongruous with a love of the earth and a workable ethical framework for the conservation thereof. The rhetoric of these causes, and the ideologies that shape such a rhetoric, are in too many instances incongruous with the self-regulating, sacrificing ethic that must lie behind an authentic respect for, and protection of, nature. In many instances, these commitments are not merely incongruous with a robust conservationism, but are in downright opposition to what we would identify as the building blocks of an authentic environmental ethic. We begin with abortion.

ABORTION AND THE EARTH

Abortion, like environmental degradation and gun violence (as two examples), is understood best as a symptom of larger systemic problems as opposed to an isolated issue. The symbiosis of abortion and poverty, for an example, is real: 42 percent of women having abortions are below the federal poverty level.[1] The high incidence of abortion (nearly one in four women

---

1. Jerman et al., "Characteristics of U.S. Abortion Patients," para. 24.

in the United States will have one by the time they reach age forty-five)[2] is a natural outcome of ideological and societal influences that degrade and devalue the human person, and perhaps most especially the female person. Our culture in general dishonors those qualities that traditionally have been equated with the feminine, such as the stable, homebound, land-bound nurture of life. When we devalue the feminine, we also devalue familial and communal relationships and obligations, natural bonds of affection, and constancy of life. Since these feminine qualities are what form and sustain households, and since households form the basis of the human community and economy, we find our economic systems likewise disfigured, along with nature itself. Traditionally, the polis (the city or the community) was referred to using feminine pronouns. This is why Christians still refer to the church as "mother." The community and its traditions of nurture is the seat of culture (from the word "cultivate," meaning to nurture and care for another). Anyone who puts forward a call to end abortion must at the same time cry out against a whole system of beliefs and actions that puts commerce before life, and the unmitigated pursuit of individual gratification and glorification before relationships of reciprocity and communal obligation. If we are to say that abortion has no place in the good society, we must also ensure that our society guards its children and its mothers, and refuses to leave them alone to contend on an economic battlefield that tends to degrade and discredit motherhood, nurture, childhood innocence, and the land itself. If we fail to do this, it would be like debating gun control and gun violence without ever mentioning our uses of media to foster and to suckle an insatiable appetite for violence, and to normalize violence as a suitable subject for entertainment and commercial venture. Why do we not hear more discussion and see more pushback against this most troubling state of affairs?

In an important and underappreciated epistemological and psychological study of the rise of modernist thought, *The Flight From Woman*, Karl Stern demonstrates that modernist philosophical systems devalue, and often couch an inherent disdain for, the qualities traditionally associated with the feminine. Modernist, rationalist thinking, argues Stern, is an unbalanced development of masculine energies and ways of knowing over the more intuitive, relational ways of coming to knowledge traditionally associated with the womanly. What is more, Stern equates ambiguity toward the feminine with ambiguity toward nature; in the literature that

---

2. "Abortion Is a Common Experience," para. 1. The number is 23.7 percent.

he analyzes, the two are synonymous.[3] It should be no surprise. We have already brought attention to the traditional intuition that identifies nature with the feminine. Indeed, our word "matter" is from the Latin root *mater*, meaning "mother." Referring to the thought of the German philosopher Arthur Schopenhauer, but highlighting a trend in all of the thinkers he scrutinizes, Stern muses,

> Ever since the birth of Jesus the mystery of love has been inextricably bound up with the mystery of the God-Man. If nature is evil *per se*, the Word cannot become Flesh. With Schopenhauer nature cannot possibly be ennobled—it can at best be negated. No blessing can ever come from motherhood, for conception and birth serve only one purpose—the perpetuation of a curse. Nothing in nature can ever partake of the redemption—this would be, in Schopenhauer's system, a contradiction in terms. No Mother can bear a Saviour. And with this Christianity must fall.[4]

As is implied in this statement, the misgiving or distrust toward nature that is prevalent in the influential thought of all of Stern's subjects expresses itself in ambiguity toward fertility, and sometimes, as in Schopenhauer's case, even an outright disgust for it. Modern feminist thinking often expresses a similar ambiguity. To be sure, when modern feminists assume that women should be equal contenders in a world dominated by fallen men, they only work in the end to exclude the feminine further and to disfigure it. It is bad enough, for example, that we shove guns into the hands of our boys and men and send them off to fight our wars. Now, in the name of inclusiveness and equality, we do the same with our girls and our women, turning those whose very biology is fashioned for the nurturing of life and culture into destroyers of these things. If we cannot value nurturing and the feminine, how can we value the earth, customarily known to be our mother?

Abortion, along with environmental degradation, has a long and sordid history, not only in the United States, but also throughout the ages of human antiquity. Far from being universally accepted and unquestioned, it was nonetheless known and practiced in ancient cultures,[5] and did not

---

3. Stern, *Flight from Woman*, 107–22. Stern includes a chapter on Descartes, Schopenhauer, Sartre, Hedda and her companions, Tolstoy, Kierkegaard, and Goethe.

4. Stern, *Flight from Woman*, 120.

5. Revisionist historian Leslie Reagan, in her book *When Abortion Was a Crime: Women, Medicine and the Law in the United States, 1867–1973*, appears to obscure or ignore the influence of religion and moral reflection on the question of abortion throughout

attract legal attention in the United States until the nineteenth century. That something is commonly practiced, however, cannot provide the basis of an argument for its moral acceptability as many proponents of abortion might suggest. For an example, the Boston Women's Health Book Collective builds an argument for abortion on the basis that "Over several centuries and in different cultures, there is a rich history of women helping each other to abort. Until the late 1800s, women healers in Western Europe and the U.S. provided abortions and trained other women to do so, without legal prohibitions."[6] Imagine if I wrote, "For centuries men have been involved in the culturally rich practice of helping men to rape women and the earth and to find convenient ways of disposing of toxic waste without concern for its effects. These industrious men have been doing so without legal prohibitions." I would hope that this argument would not fly. Perhaps the desire to limit abortion by making it illegal except in extreme cases is a sign of human progress. Just because people commonly over-harvest resources and broadcast pollutants into the environment does not mean that these practices are ethical and do not necessitate legal attention for the sake of the common good. Besides this, a multitude is capable of shared insanity and of doing great evil, a point to which not only many conservationists but human rights activists as well should be sympathetic. Herein lies the Achilles' heel of democracy itself. Can a practice be said to be morally and ethically appropriate by sole virtue of the fact that a majority of people accept and do it? Any sound inquiry into ethics demands an appeal to an objective reality beyond personal opinions and feelings. For conservation, as for abortion, the reality to which we must appeal is nature itself.

In 1821, Connecticut was the first state to limit abortion by law, specifically illegalizing abortions practiced after "quickening," a relatively subjective term indicating the time when the fetus was felt to be moving. In 1875, the prototypical women's suffragist Susan B. Anthony ranked abortion among the great evils of society in a speech entitled "Social Purity."

---

history. She fails to recognize that ancient Christian witness alone, in texts that we have dating back at least to the second century, is unanimous in its denouncement of abortion as synonymous with murder. She also fails to note the practice of many ancient Christians of saving and raising infants who had been exposed (left to die), which was a relatively common practice, but by no means a celebrated one, in the Roman Empire. Because a certain practice is prevalent does not mean that it is an ethical or desirable one, or something to be celebrated. Cf. Ravitz, "Surprising History of Abortion," and Gorman, "Abortion and the Early Church."

6. *Our Bodies, Ourselves*, 388.

Such evils, as she said it, were the result of man's dominance over woman. She believed that the "liberation" of women—that is, women having an equal status to men in the social and political sphere—would lead to social purity.[7] Then, crimes against humanity such as infanticide and abortion would no longer stain our civilization. Anthony based her argument for equal rights for women in the assumption that a woman, perhaps more than a man, would use these rights to give and to nourish life, to uphold fidelity and accountability for all.

It was the American Medical Association that forwarded statutes that led to the illegalization of abortion in 1890, excepting in cases where the mother's life was at stake. In 1916, Margaret Sanger, a feminist of her own time who demonstrates a rather different approach than that of her forerunner Anthony, founded Planned Parenthood. Sanger, along with the institution that continues to carry on her work, fought a painstaking and effective crusade to reverse the relatively newly established laws that sought to place limits on the occurrence of abortion, seeking not only to legalize but also to popularize both contraception and abortion. Sanger was not only a proponent of the casual sexual encounter for all, but of eugenics, the science of improving the human population by a program of controlled breeding (a science the Nazis sought to perfect). To have both free sex and controlled breeding together necessitated the use of contraception and, when contraception failed, abortion. "Planned Parenthood," reads the "Our History" page of the organization's website, "traces its roots back to nurse, educator and founder Margaret Sanger—whose activism changed the world. Sanger had the revolutionary idea that women should control their own bodies—and thus their own destinies. Imagine that!"[8]

The question before us in this chapter is not necessarily the question about the legalization of abortion. Legal or illegal, we are interested in an ethic that would inform virtuous choices made in freedom, as is the ultimate task with conservation and land use. Our task, then, is to examine the rhetoric that so often attends the arguments that bolster abortion not only as a legal option, but as a viable and essentially amoral (or even a morally correct) one. More to the point, our burden is to question an understanding of abortion as an issue wholly disconnected from the issue of conservation, and to discern if the rhetoric regarding the one supports or undermines the logic regarding the other.

7. Anthony, "Social Purity."
8. "Our History," para. 1.

The first bit of rhetoric we will look at is the pro-choice argument that focuses on individual rights and freedoms, an argument that ironically echoes the very same idiom taken up by those in opposition to laws that seek to protect the environment. We have already explored the tapered ways in which contemporary Americans conceive of rights, and must keep this discussion in mind as we go forward. As the argument goes, a woman has the right not to have someone else's will imposed on her body without her choice. When it comes to murder, abuse, and rape, for three examples, who can argue with this? Each of these examples seeks to protect the integrity of a woman's body. The argument as applied to abortion, however, protects a woman's right to despoil her own body. The argument is twofold: The State, through the law (or other people in their busybody moralizing), is perceived as imposing its will on the woman's body by limiting her choice when it comes to abortion. In addition, the fetus itself is perceived as somehow imposing something on the woman's body. A fetus, like a rapist, does not possess the right to use this woman's body for its own ends. An infant is wholly dependent on its mother, but we must ask if that gives the mother a right to destroy it? There are a host of citizens wholly dependent on others for their survival—children, the elderly, the handicapped—but does that mean that we have a right to destroy them? I am wholly dependent on the farmer for my food; does this mean that she has the right to destroy me because I have some kind of claim on her life, because I am little more than a parasite, a mere tick on her leg? Who is not wholly dependent on others? Not a one. Who has absolute rights in a symbiotic world? Only tyrants. Ecological thinking compels us to make these conclusions.

To admit that the fetus is using the mother's body, however, is to admit that the fetus has a life of its own apart from the mother—that it is somehow a distinct life—and that concession leads us into some murky moral ground. The other angle of the argument, then, underplays this distinction. Because the fetus cannot live apart from the mother, it is not really a life apart from its mother. The mother, therefore, has the right to do what she wants with this fetus that is really nothing more than an extension of her own self, her own ego, her own will, her own choosing, her own body. To remove it is no more a problem than popping a zit, or removing a tumor, or an eyeball, or a breast.

The most disappointing features of rights-based arguments in general is an artificial focus on individuals as opposed to a more realistic focus on relationships, a point that we have already begun to explore in the previous chapter. While I may be free to do whatever I will, I have to admit that not everything that I do is good. While I have the right to have ownership of private property, this does not mean that I have the right to misuse it, especially because my property, like my body, is connected to other properties. My activities on the land that I own by right will affect others. Arguments from rights as we currently perceive them—be they arguments about abortion, marriage, or guns—fail to address communal dependencies. They speak of the human person as if the human person were a self-existent, atomized entity. Not one of us is self-existent; this is the first principle of religion, ecology, and sound ethics. We are all dependent, contingent, and so are restricted as to the breadth of our autonomy. This means that there are no absolute human rights, not one, especially if we are thinking about these rights as belonging to isolated individuals with the purpose of maximizing individual choice and entitlement rather than as protections that we share in common. I am not saying that individual human beings do not have tremendous value. I am only saying that our rights (to the extent that we perceive rights as entitlements that belong to segregated individuals) are limited, as our lives are limited, by relationship. It is this way by nature. Especially if we are to enjoy any of the fruits of civilization, our rights (or the exercise of our rights) must be limited and conditional.

An incessant appeal to rights, then, is inherently flawed. It betrays our lack of any probing consideration of the network of relationships and dependencies within and by which we have existence, including a consideration of the government that affirms and safeguards rights. Just as we conceive of a fetus apart from the relationship that produces it, so we conceive of rights apart from the community within which they are realized. Alone on a desert island, there is no need of rights. There, there are no rights, for wind and rain, hunger and thirst: these care little for our perceived entitlements. In community, where the abuse of power is likely and the balance between liberty and a common good is necessary, there are rights. Unfortunately, so-called pro-life arguments run along the same flawed lines when they seek to extend the "right to life" to an atomized fetus. Such arguments do little or nothing to bring to light a broader context within which we might address the real questions at stake when it comes to pregnancy and abortion. It would do us well to move beyond our blind appeal to individual rights and rather to focus more clearly on the relational character of our lives, our actions, our choices. We might then ask ourselves how behaviors and attitudes not only shape individuals, but society and the land itself. I do not here advocate the destruction of the individual for the sake of some whole, for nothing is whole without all of its parts. Rather, I advocate an ethically considered exercise of our unique personhood within the larger contexts of our lives, in all possible instances tempered and directed by the deepening of authentic love. If not this, then informed by sound law and a government unafraid to guide her people to higher roads rather than making standards out of what are instead the lowest common denominators or, worse yet, nothing common at all, just an appeal to atomized, individual choices and expediencies. Where there is no love, no fidelity, no sacrifice made in freedom, there must be law.

When we apply this to the argument of a woman's right to do what she pleases with the body that belongs to her, we must begin by understanding her pregnancy itself as a communal phenomenon. Indeed, the whole endeavor of raising a child, from start to finish, is a communal phenomenon. No woman should be left to do it alone. Indeed, no nuclear family should be left to do it alone. It takes an extended family, a village, a nation. Nature takes for granted that pregnancy is not an isolated matter, but occurs within an ecosystem of relationships: male and female, clan, community, the land itself. When a woman is pregnant, she has already given her body over to the use of another. She is by this time intimately involved with another life in an act that has never not been an act of union and begetting, the latter at least in potential. Our belief that sex can be casual, like sipping a glass of wine on a summer evening, is wholly in opposition to this fact, as it is in opposition to nature itself. We even acknowledge that sipping a glass of wine on a summer evening is not casual if one is prone to sipping too much wine or if one is about to jump into their car and drive down a road shared by others. The idea that sex can be casual is one of the pernicious lies that we have happily bought into, that we should be able to use sex for our own purposes and pleasures wholly apart from its natural potentialities and principles, apart from its natural power. This lie is foundational to Margaret Sanger's work and the work of Planned Parenthood. Technology makes the disconnect possible, even believable, as it makes it possible for me to forget that, when I turn up the heat to keep myself warm, I am participating in a vast network of fossil fuel extraction. When I believe that the land I own can be used for my own purposes and pleasures apart from the potential or actual results of those purposes and pleasures, am I not essentially operating under the same assumptions? I am exercising what I believe is my right, but according to a false understanding of the nature of the act itself and wholly inconsiderate of the context within which I do it. Planned Parenthood's website boasts that the organization "was founded on the revolutionary idea that women should have the information and care they need to live strong, healthy lives and fulfill their dreams—no ceilings, no limits."[9] We will see this false promise of "no ceilings, no limits" time and again in this work, and how destructive it is to stable human society and how radically it undermines conservation. It is shocking to me that we have so wholeheartedly bought into this rhetoric of personal freedom when it comes to sex, an intrinsically communal act so charged by nature with significance and purpose, and fail to see its relationship to an ethic of respect for the limitations of nature that would govern a sound conservationist position. To exploit the good things of nature to our own insular ends and for our own blinkered pleasure is always potentially hazardous, be it our own bodies, the bodies of others, or the body of the earth.

Some might argue that the risks involved in pregnancy justify abortion. Though pregnancy does pose a very real threat to the mother, insofar as childbirth and pregnancy complications can cause death, pregnancy is not, however, a sickness. In America, "pregnancy complications" are the sixth leading cause of death among women twenty to thirty-four years of age, consisting of 2.8 percent of all women in this age group who die. To put this in perspective, "unintentional injuries" is the leading cause of death among women ages twenty to thirty-four, at 35.9 percent.[10] To be sure, the very nature of pregnancy is that it demands something not only of women, but also of men and society as a whole. It demands the most of women, however, on both a physical and emotional level. To purchase a houseplant, to plant a garden, to raise a cat or chickens or a dog, all of this requires that we show up to care for these various lives that depend on us for their survival. Our lives are changed by these commitments; our narrow ideas of liberty are threatened. Taking on a child brings this to a whole other level, to be sure, but perhaps only in degree. Might we often be a little too uptight about raising children? Is it possible to take it too seriously? We tend to miss the playfulness and joy in caring for another life, in this relationship of dependence. All around us we are told by the marketers and the sellers that we need this and that for our children, that they must have the very best that money can buy—the best homes, the best toys, the best parents, the best therapists, the best healthcare, the best education. If they cannot,

9. "Who We Are," para. 1.
10. "Leading Causes of Death in Females," fig. 1.

they are better off never having lived, as I suppose all the poor of the world are better off not living. If we have bought into this line of thinking, has not the market won? If the market has won, has not conservation then lost? I know a mother who, when she found that she was pregnant, moved into a small cabin without electricity to raise her child. She did a decent job at it, too, saying that it was the best experience of her life. I do not know where the father was, and surely her raising the child alone was not ideal, but she did it, made the most of it, and has never looked back.

Another alleged risk that abortion can help to reduce, as the argument goes, is that of shame and conflict when the woman in unmarried. Having an abortion can save a woman from having to stand up to others who might mistreat her because of her pregnancy. The stigma borne by single mothers is not nearly as severe as it once may have been. Indeed, 39.8 percent of all births in the United States are to unmarried women, so unmarried mothers are in good company.[11] Support can be found if sought, even when others are hostile. Yes, the inherent risks of pregnancy are reduced by the possibility of abortion. This goes without saying. We must ask, however, if the avoidance of risk despite the costs is a behavior worth encouraging. We must wonder if it is beneficial to the advancement of life to seek to live risk-free, burden-free, free of the perceived shackles of caring for another, or even if it is possible or realistic to expect to live this way. After all, did not someone give birth to each of us?

From an ecological perspective, it is clear that one life begets another for the sake of the life begotten. While the life begotten takes life in order to live, there are limits to its taking. It must eventually offer itself back for the sake of another. The fruitfulness of nature always demands this give-and-take, this coincident interplay of survival and sacrifice. Our own lives are upheld by countless fatalities, by countless martyrdoms. We walk on the backs of the dead. When we reflect on this, we realize (perhaps not without some angst) that the eventual giving of our own lives is part and parcel to the plan of nature. It is inevitable. At the very core of the nature of things, a necessity for all that is contingent and finite, is the fact that life is sustained by sacrifice. It was once considered more appropriate, in the face of this reality, for a person to choose to make the sacrifice herself rather than to require the sacrifice of another. In the protection of one's country and community, in the protection of one's spouse and friends, in the protection of one's children, in the protection of the land, a person commendably met

---

11. "Unmarried Childbearing," para. 3.

whatever challenge was at hand by offering his or her own life—through their work and sometimes through their death—for the sake of a larger reality. Perhaps such a sentiment is old-fashioned, but the fact remains that, in some instances, the moral imperative demands a decision either to give of oneself, or to require that another make this sacrifice for us. It is a humbling catch-22. As far as the environment is concerned, no conservation effort would be complete without a strong emphasis on voluntary sacrifice. To embrace conservation is to accept our due share in the sacrifices that life requires. We are asked to sacrifice conveniences, profits, comforts, freedoms. We are asked to not demand that the other be our holocaust at no cost to ourselves, or, worse, to our own profit. Conservation's aim is to provide an ethical narrative that will encourage such bravery, that we not require a total sacrifice of the earth and its non-human creatures for the sake of our own ventures, however respectable these ventures may be. In the end, the distinction is a sham, for sacrificing earth to our ends means that it is we who are sacrificed, just as a mother sacrificing a fetus means that the mother is sacrificed. We are among the creatures of the earth. As her creatures, she has a claim on our lives. Who can live without the earth? Are we not all just fetuses? A human mother who has taken real risks for her children has, in return, a claim on her children. They, too, must sacrifice for her. She is not required to be perfect in every way—which is an impossibility—nor is she required to be wealthy, to provide for her children all of the toys and experiences that they might demand and that other mothers may shower on their children, nor even must she provide her children with the best healthcare or a college education. She is only to give her best according to the resources available to her; having done that, she has been the best mother anyone can be. This holds true for the fathers, as well.

We have stated before that Margaret Sanger, celebrated founder of Planned Parenthood, was committed to eugenics. The principles of eugenics were considered with relative ease by many before the Nazis' practices exposed the grave dangers inherent in them. For example, Teddy Roosevelt attacked the act of using birth control as "criminal against the race." His point was that, when women of the dominant race and classes (educated northern Europeans) did not reproduce, they would soon be eclipsed by the poor foreigners who did reproduce. Such an approach to eugenics sought to maintain the balance between the "fit" and the "unfit" by ensuring that the "fit" produced offspring.[12] Today, we hear similar concerns expressed in

---

12. "Fit" and "unfit" were quasi-technical terms in the literature of eugenics.

European democratic countries where the birthrate of Muslim immigrants, for an example, far outstrips the birthrate of native Europeans. The threat that these countries may quickly but imperceptibly become Muslim countries is indeed quite real. In such a case, Roosevelt would urge the natives to have children. Sanger's approach was different. Hers was to limit the reproduction of the unfit through contraception and, when that failed, abortion. The approach found support, as it allowed the affluent, educated elite to continue to pursue their careers and pleasures without the responsibilities of family life even though they, too, were alarmed by the high birth rates among the poor and working classes. The fecundity of these latter groups, so thought Sanger and as she herself put it, was "the most far-reaching peril to the future of civilization."[13] A motivating factor in Sanger's push for contraception and, when contraception failed, abortion, was driven by these considerations. She even advocated that people apply for a license from the government to reproduce, an idea that has borne fruit in present day China. Talk about a government impingement on one's body!

COOL WATER

All of this is to raise the question about how we talk about, think about, and use the things that supposedly belong to us. This is, of course, one of the major questions of conservation, and it is at the heart of a true conservation ethic. If we are to demonstrate a way forward for the conservation of our land, can we do so while engaging in rhetoric about other supposedly unrelated issues that, in essence, follows the exact same logical lines of those who oppose environmental considerations? As people who are concerned for the earth, we must take our own assumptions and logic to task for the sake of the earth. And, for the sake of the earth, we must abandon, renounce, sacrifice the skewed rhetorical lines that would assert that we are nothing but isolated individuals whose private choices do not and cannot affect the whole. Such a way of thinking runs entirely against the grain of a sound, ecologically based environmentalism. Just as the land community is interconnected, so is the human community—body, mind, and soul. This works the other way round, as well. If we are to highlight the relational aspects of pregnancy in an effort to curb abortion, we must then be willing to apply these very same principals to our uses of the land and the proliferation of guns, for two examples. If we are to criticize laissez-faire

13. Sanger, *Pivot of Civilization*, 127.

morality when it comes to sex, we must also criticize it when it comes to the marketplace. There are no private choices when we are in relationship. Just as laissez-faire sexuality does not regulate itself, but instead leads to chaos and degeneration, so does laissez-faire economics. Does this mean that the government should control all of our choices? Absolutely not! Does this mean that we should have no sense of boundary to our lives? Absolutely not! I am deeply troubled by the incessant connectivity and resultant loss of personal boundary that our current uses of technology have encouraged. Still, our relationships are concrete, and hence it is love that should govern our choices and our uses of the good things of this life, including our bodies, our land, and our technologies. Our uses of these must be informed and directed by a mature recognition and acceptance of the limiting reality of the relationships in which our lives are embedded. But, when love is abandoned, we must turn to government.

If we cannot say that abortion is clearly immoral (that it is murder, quite simply), we are compelled to all admit that abortion is certainly morally charged. Unclear as to what the role of government might be in legislating such a deeply moral decision, and taking seriously evidence that bans on abortion effect women very unequally, often on lines of race or class (wealthy women can simply travel to another state or country to get an abortion), we might affirm it as a legal option for everyone in every case with the compromise limitations specified in *Roe v. Wade*. Nevertheless, government, even when leaving certain choices open to individual conscience, has a duty to guide her people to the higher roads, the same roads that will foster not only self-controlled individuals, but the well-ordered society that such individuals will together create. In this case, the way that affirms life, personal responsibility, and strong family bonds seems to be the path that government should persuade her people to take—if not by law then by example and by where it puts its resources. What too often happens is the reverse: equality, understood as "social justice" rather than as a fundamental equality before the law, means sacrificing the higher way for the sake of a lower way so that no one feels disadvantaged or challenged.[14]

---

14. For an example of this kind of approach, often forwarded by the extreme Left, see Brighouse and Swift, *Family Values*. Brighouse and Swift, in their narrow idea of equality, suggest that parents who spend time reading to their children at bedtime might be giving their children an unfair advantage over those whose parents do not. Quality time spent with children, then, becomes a moral dilemma. This patently absurd suggestion can lead to a conclusion as dangerous as it is lazy: that perhaps the best way to achieve social equality is to suppress the family altogether. This is, of course, a very Marxist resolution

Imagine if environmentalists took this approach. Imagine suggesting that we lower environmental standards so that the worst polluters do not feel left out, disadvantaged, or challenged in any way. At the same time, the government must be willing to put its money where its mouth is. In its role of calling us to greatness of virtue, government must also provide the necessary supports to make this greatness possible. These include access to education, health care, and support for mothers who have been willing to sacrifice for their children without other family supports, such as a responsible husband. This is especially critical in a time when the individualist, industrialist, global endeavor—enhanced by governmental policy and the media—has so thoroughly eroded normative grassroots support networks. While governments should not be in the business of funding abortions, they should be in the business of assisting women and couples who have chosen not to have one. At the very least, any government worth its salt cannot talk about all choices as if they were equal. There are good choices and bad choices; wise choices and evil choices; choices driven by narcissism and vice, and choices that build virtue; choices that break societal bonds and choices that bolster them.

As such, it would do environmentalists well, in my estimation, to distance themselves from the rhetoric of laissez-faire sex and absolutist claims to fetuses and even our own bodies. It would do us well to encourage sacrifice and care for another, personal responsibility, and a sound respect for the natural bounds and aims of the sexual act. Otherwise, how shall we convince others to make sacrifices for sea turtles, or a certain kind of bird, frog, plant, or rock formation? How will we convince someone of the interconnectedness of nature when we are defending our own disconnectedness? How shall we talk about the sanctity of nature when we ourselves are willing and ready to desecrate our own bodies? Why is it not okay for a landowner to pierce the earth with a fracking rig to extract natural gas, but fine to pierce a woman's womb to extract a child? Should we not rather demonstrate to the world that we ourselves are willing to give a little on the notion of private ownership and an appeal to the supposed harmlessness of private choices? Certainly, if we take ecology seriously, we cannot take these kinds of arguments seriously. To further them only stokes the fires of individualism run amok, the very fires that we need to be throwing cool water on.

---

to the perceived problem of inequality. Why not hold the good parents up before all, that their behaviors and their choices may become a model for society?

Chapter 5

The Moral Logic of Conservation: LGBTQ Narratives and the Love of Nature

> To change ideas about what land is for is to change ideas about what anything is for. Thus we started to move a straw, and end up with the job of moving a mountain.[1]
>
> —Aldo Leopold

It is a clear February day, the kind that makes the maple sap and the blood run with vigor. To not take to the trail on a day like this, especially after the seemingly unending succession of winter-gray days, would be to squander a great gift. Toil and ambition are the best things to forsake; let the wind take them away! Let the wind buffet against the cheeks, chilly and bracing, like a spray of clear, living water. Let the wind baptize anew. In the distance, perfectly framed in spruce and the falling slopes of forested hillsides, the blue and purple crests of these ancient hills are like the Rubenesque lines of a reclining, comely dame. Though comely, though reclining, detached and inviolate, as chaste as a child. The desire to possess or exploit would cast a pall over delighted eyes. It would be to go blind. In this way, soft and yielding under the feet, the path leads on from glory to glory. To follow it is to drink deeply of life.

1. Leopold, "State of the Profession," 280.

THE MYTH OF THE LIMITLESSNESS OF THE LIMITED

Bowers suggests that it is time to stop taking self-proclaimed "conservatives" at their word. Rush Limbaugh, William F. Buckley Jr., and organizations such as the wise use movement masquerade their liberalism and libertarianism under the pretext of being "conservative." What is more confusing is that Buckley, while identifying himself as a conservative, at times also referred to himself as a libertarian.[2] It is hard to reconcile these two claims, as their underlying assumptions arise from two very different sets of values. Buckley's ease in placing them side by side demonstrates loud and clear the confused political language and moral assumptions of our age. The interests of local communities and economies, the interests of self-sufficiency apart from foreign dependencies, the concern to maintain the integrity of families and the traditions passed down through them, are all conservative concerns. Bowers laments that

> self-proclaimed liberals have sat in the same university classrooms as the self-proclaimed conservatives who are now promoting the WTO and the globalization of a consumer-style monoculture. Both groups, along with others . . . listened to professors who were indifferent to the importance of rectifying our use of political language. As long as this indifference persists within our educational institutions and within the general public, the Limbaughs and Wise Use advocates of the world will continue to exploit a gullible public in a linguistic double bind.[3]

In other words, we will continue to masquerade what is essentially liberal and libertarian as "conservative," while environmentalists themselves will continue to confuse their essentially conservative task as a liberal agenda, locking arms with the very forces that would undermine their work.

The fourth article of belief of the so-called wise use movement—summed up by Ron Arnold in his paper entitled "Wise Use: What Do We Believe?"—is that "Our limitless imaginations can break through natural limits to make earthly goods and carrying capacity virtually limitless."[4] We have heard this idea expressed before and in many forms. As we have

---

2. See, for an example, the title of Buckley's book, *Happy Days Were Here Again: Reflections of a Libertarian Journalist.*

3. Bowers, *Mindful Conservatism*, 66.

4. Quoted in Bowers, *Mindful Conservatism*, 54.

already said, such an idea is liberal and libertarian at its heart. To question the ethical validity of these "limitless" imaginings, or to wonder whether or not, if put into practice, they might undermine human communities, disempower a community's ability to self-regulate and so self-limit, erode its ability to remain self-sufficient and independent of unhealthy global and commercial dependencies, and degrade the lands on which this sufficiency depends, would be conservative. The liberal belief in so-called limitless human imaginations that can break all natural limitations not only drives the globalization of markets, but is carried over into contemporary reflections about sex, family, and gender, with the results that we would expect from such an ideology. We presently turn our attention to this in order to demonstrate that LGBTQ storylines often advance the same libertarian narratives that undergird the wise use movement's anti-environmental stance, the erudite so-called conservatism of Buckley, and the populist piss and vinegar of Limbaugh.

I can already predict that many will find my focus on LGBTQ suppositions objectionable and unfair. What has this to do with conservation? My answer to this question, and the answer as far as the majority of the public is concerned, is "just about everything." LGBTQ movements have gained much prominence over many years of concerted, organized effort. They are supported lock, stock, and barrel, with little to no critical thought, by the Left, who also have taken upon themselves the environmental cause. A critical examination of the underlying worldviews and moral assumptions commonly advanced by these constituencies, especially as they relate to the moral values and assumptions that would foster a strong conservation ethic, is long overdue, given our propensity to place them cheek to cheek as two equal causes. This chapter, like the one preceding it, is imperative because of the alliance of environmentalism with the LGBTQ agendas, if not by design then by default and association. If I vote for the environment, I am also voting to promote these special interest groups. In the public mind, at least, and in the ballot booth, to forward one is to forward another.

It is true that this chapter might nearly just as well have focused on the broader issue of the so-called sexual revolution, advanced by the liberal agenda and of which the LGBTQ itineraries form a part. A large portion of the burden of this chapter has to do with the assumptions behind laissez-faire sexual pursuit and the removal of the human sexual act from the sphere, not only of human obligations and relationships, but from its larger biological context.⁵ LGBTQ narratives, however, jump from the proverbial frying pan into the fire when they do not stop there but further seek to remove the human person herself from her embeddedness in the gendered correlations of nature. Please note that I take up the LGBTQ agendas, as I have called them, as social, theoretical, and political movements. I by no means imply that every person who identifies with one or more of these groups forwards the claims that I herein highlight, nor am I unaware of the internal conflicts within this group that might make the use of the term a little misrepresentative.⁶ The acronym "LGBTQ" includes within itself a wide range of constituencies and identities. Sexual preference and gender uncertainties seem the common denominator. We are led to think that LGBTQ is a single constituency or movement seeking a unified end, but this is not always the case. Lesbians and gays have been in conflict, accusations of classism and racism are flung about within the ranks of these populations, while many lesbians and gays feel that various transgender agendas are incongruent with their own cause, for a few examples. Then there are the "queers," who often seem content to be just that. Because of this, I refer to LGBTQ "agendas," "narratives," "movements," and so forth in the plural rather than as a singular, monolithic constituency.

Like the previous chapter, I focus on LGBTQ movements in an effort to convict and convince serious-minded environmentalists to make for some clear distance between LGBTQ causes and the environmental imperative, a distance that is very difficult to forge amidst the whirlwinds of emotion and manipulation that have whipped up such a dense froth around LGBTQ issues. Like narratives surrounding abortion, LGBTQ advocates rely on the liberal and libertarian assumptions that propel a laissez-faire market and its culture of exploitation and consumption. They rely on the supposition that persons are autonomous individuals whose rights have little more meaning than the amplification of self-contained choices and predilections. They rely on the view that all change is progress and therefore requires little deliberation about linkages and continuity with the past or long-term future

---

5. Suggestions have been made that environmentalism will only take hold if it is given more sex appeal. Our society needs "to be persuaded that ecology can be sexy, and not self-denying." We are told of the "hedonism that environmentalist politics so desperately needs for it to be populist and libertarian" (Kerridge, "Environmentalism and Ecocriticism," 534).

6. The Wikipedia article on the term "LGBT" highlights some of these conflicts. Note the almost endless parsing of specialized identity groups that serves to undermine a common goal between them. See "LGBT," https://en.wikipedia.org/wiki/LGBT.

consequences, and they forward their causes in a spirit of disparagement and disdain for traditional norms, stabilizing institutions, and communal relationships of obligation, deeming them repressive and backwards. Our efforts are, at the same time, aimed at those who may view the environmental cause with suspicion because of its political alliance with LGBTQ agendas, demonstrating that they are not only not the same, but that they spring from cultural and moral assumptions that are often conflicting. Perhaps there can be more bipartisan support on issues of conservation if we can approach conservation on its own terms, apart from its current political bedfellows and confused political language. To do this is to consider conservation from a more morally reliable place. Provided that we can at least, in its outlines, agree about the ethical commitments that would make for a sensible and authentic environmentalism, we might then assess other issues according to the same moral logic.

In accordance with the designs of LGBTQ movements, the act of critiquing them is progressively becoming an absolute taboo. It is therefore all the more important to critique them, especially when many (not all) of the underlying ideologies that drive and nourish them are malignant not only toward society, but toward nature. Such ideologies are in conflict with the values that would foster respect for a settled life, rooted in the land community and willingly limited by the bounds of the natural world. Many of these ideologies are in fact disdainful of such a life, and would rather work to presuade us and our children away from it at all costs. You may not in the end agree with all of my points and assessments, which are admittedly stated in no uncertain terms, and this chapter (like the rest of this work) will certainly miss some of the shades of grey that daub all issues. Perhaps all of us know and like LGBTQ individuals. I as much as any would love to just say "live and let live" and be done with it. I would most assuredly never condone violence or acts of hatred against these or any other groups; all of us live by grace and none of us are unbroken. Still, if we care for the environment, I think it is important to be able to examine and discuss with frankness and candor at least some of the more extreme ideologies that have bolstered LGBTQ agendas. If we cannot do this, we do not live in a democracy. Like it or not, here to stay or no, these ideologies are having a profound influence on our culture; we are all affected by them. Critiquing and discussing these issues is important in light of the emotional and ideological headlock that LGBTQ movements currently have us in and, most importantly for our purposes, their current political association with the environmental cause.

THE ARGUMENT FROM HISTORY

Like members of many movements, both honorable and dodgy, LGBTQ advocates look to history to find ancient precedence for their cause. Pagan Greek and Roman mythologies yield good results, or so it seems, but one finds examples of homoerotic practice in all cultures, which should not surprise anyone. We should note that these examples often intertwine homoerotic practice with acts of pedophilia, especially with boys, noting also that so-called homoerotic sentiments are found by its supporters in places where they likely do not lie, such as in certain literary descriptions of the beauty of a young boy. A writer may think many things are beautiful, children included.

In the end, such arguments from history are rickety. We could just as easily focus on the Greco-Roman obsession with celibacy and virginity, shared by many other cultures. Indeed, this is a value that we would do well to advance for its bearing on earth-care and the setting aside of tracts of land as untouched, virgin wilderness. We are thus bound to make a similar conclusion when it comes to the use and expression of sexual energy in general. If we are to assert that nature and her energies are sacred and so require a use that is tempered with respect, care, and a sense of responsibility that puts bounds on that use, then we have to assert the same when it comes to the use of sexual energy. Why would we call for the conservation and right use of our energy resources while thinking it is okay to squander and casually misuse our sexual energies? The ancient and great philosophers and religious teachers in the Greco-Roman world (and generally historically in nearly all cultures) tell of the need to limit and direct the use of such energies with discipline and respect. The Roman historian and Latin literary stylist Sallust (c. 86–c. 34 BC) and many others like him provide other important historical voices that we cannot responsibly just brush aside. Praising the statesman Marcus Cato (234–149 BC), Sallust quotes Cato as having said,

> Do not imagine that it was by force of arms that our ancestors made the republic great from its small beginnings. If that were true, we would have a far more excellent republic now than they did then. Indeed, we are far better supplied with allies, citizens, arms,

and horses than they were. But it was other qualities that made them great, qualities which are wholly lacking in us: diligence at home, just rule abroad, and an independent spirit in counsel, addicted neither to crime nor to lust. Instead of these, what we have is self-indulgence and greed, public impoverishment and private wealth. We praise riches, we live for idleness, we make no distinction between good people and bad, and raw ambition usurps all the rewards that virtue ought to have. And it is no wonder—when each of you takes thought only for himself, when you are slaves to pleasure at home and to money and favor here in public—that any assault would come on a republic that has no defenses.[7]

As far as the argument from history goes, LGBTQ culling of historical evidence to support the acceptability and normativity of their various sexual itineraries is, in fact, invalidated by their simultaneous lament about the long history of persecution suffered by LGBTQ people. If the latter is the case, then it was never popularly or widely accepted or practiced, as anyone with just the very least amount of education well knows. We have to conclude, in any case, that history provides us a very mixed bag. To be sure, it is not even an equally mixed bag. As far as finding a standard for what is normative from history, heterosexuals quite obviously and unsurprisingly win the day, especially when it comes to marriage across all cultures and times. Still, anyone can glean through history and find ammunition there to bolster his or her position; we are not saved by historical unanimity from having to make a moral assessment now. As we have already established in the previous chapter, arguments for support from history, though powerful and important, cannot substantiate aptness. As any good conservationist should know, human cultures are fallen. We have a long history of violence, perversion, and abuse of the land under our belts. Vast amounts of land wasted by pollution, a river that burns, great garbage swills in our seas extending twice the square mileage of Texas—does the historical evidence of such things make them desirable or right, something not only to tolerate or accept in our own time, but also to celebrate?

To further this point even more, there is much historical and anthropological evidence, even in artwork, of the ancient practice of bestiality. It is depicted in prehistoric rock paintings, in Greek mythological literature, on ancient Roman oil lamps, right up to our time in films, magazines, and websites. It has a long history in law, being at times and in places outlawed

---

7. Sallust, *Cataline Conspiracy*, 52; quoted in Augustine of Hippo, *City of God*, 162.

and in other times and places decriminalized.[8] A 2013 WebProNews.com article reports on a zoophile rights march that happened in Berlin.[9] Since 1969, bestiality was not considered illegal in Germany, but in 2012 lawmakers were considering placing a ban on the practice. The zoophile community organized itself, filing suit against the government with the claim that a law against bestiality would violate their rights. The article continues,

> A few months later, the folks at ZETA, a German zoophile-rights group, put together a peaceful protest/march that would make its way through the street of Berlin. The group used the march to highlight the persecution that zoophiles face every day. The civil rights group, Equality for All, showed up to the protest as well.[10]

If they keep at it, perhaps someday they will be able to marry their hamsters, dogs, and sheep.

So much for arguments from history, and so much for arguments from rights. We are interested in what clear bounds, what measures and standards, will make for healthy human communities free to form not only their presents, but also their futures, without wasting their substance (including the substance of the land) on what is trivial, or on the evanescent indulgences of every whim that might present itself.

Branding LGBTQ constituencies as a singular persecuted community is powerful, persuasive, effective, and not entirely without merit. They have endured much ill treatment, and continue to endure it. But where are the limits of these kinds of identifications? That there can be a zoophile rights group who can gain the support of other rights groups with the claim that they are marginalized by society, is not only troubling. It demonstrates loud and clear our ill-conceived notion of rights and the power of the rhetoric of victimhood that can so easily overwhelm the already weakened emotional and intellectual integrity of a media-impaled public.

---

8. "History of Zoophilia," https://en.wikipedia.org/wiki/History_of_zoophilia.

9. "Zoophiles March on Berlin," https://www.webpronews.com/zoophiles-march-on-berlin-to-demand-equal-rights/. A medical definition of zoophilia is a sexual disorder involving an erotic attraction to animals or an abnormal desire to have sexual contact with animals.

10. "Zoophiles March on Berlin," para. 2.

CULTURE AND THE AGRICULTURE OF THE HEART

Truth-telling forms the core of the LGBTQ rhetoric of "coming-out." No doubt, truth-telling is a moral good. Anyone who has ever told even a close friend in confidence something that has gnawed away at them in the isolation of secrets knows how freeing and gracious truth-telling can be—if, that is, there is a compassionate ear to receive it. LGBTQ persons often vividly describe the internal conflicts caused by the painful and confusing whirlwind of passions and perceptions that they experience. Admitting these candidly can be freeing and healing, and a society where such things can be spoken about openly, provided that these things can also be seriously considered, is a society that I want to live in. Nevertheless, we must also openly admit that just because certain passions and perceptions exist, just because we struggle with and experience them, does not mean that they need to or should be celebrated, or that we should build not only our personal lives and identities around them, but also a whole society. There are many outcomes to truth-telling, and these largely have to do with the role of the listener. In an AA meeting, for example, one admits her loss of control over the desire and passion for alcohol. Though the AA community listens not only with compassion and empathy, but also from a place of identity, their role as listener is to support the person in overcoming the addiction, not to drink a toast to it. Other forums of so-called truth-telling encourage the opposite, such as a zoophile confessing his secrets to other zoophiles in an online chatroom, where he finds support for, and learns to feel good about, his tragic perversion.

 Ethical traditions communicate the need to discipline and properly direct our passions, sometimes even to put them to death. Spiritual teachers from many traditions have told us that, when our passions direct us, we are as good as enslaved to them. Like a rider and a horse, like a captain and a ship, we must be their governors rather than allowing them to govern us. In a false sense of democracy that presents all things as essentially equal, we have not only been led to believe that allowing the free rein of our passions is one and the same as liberty, but we construct whole identities around them. In doing so, we reduce the dignity of our humanity to an appetite, opinion, preference, or orientation. Some would rather see people as persons with all of the living mystery and freedom of will that that word entails, not as identities. We can become so dominated and driven by our passions—and this includes heterosexual lust—that we feel ourselves to be the victims of the things that rouse them, such as a rapist blaming the woman he rapes for his actions. How is this freedom?

The federalist contributor Dan McLaughlin gives a sane, detailed, and compassionate account of the effects of LGBTQ agendas on religious liberty in a five-part series of articles that ran in 2015. Citing a study by the Center for Disease Control, McLaughlin notes the following:

> Nearly a third of the people who self-identify as either gay or bisexual consider themselves bisexual. Whether or not you believe that people are born bisexual, it is ridiculous to suggest that bisexuality offers no choice. If you're going to accept the monogamy inherent in marriage, you must suppress your attraction either towards the opposite sex or towards your own sex.[11]

The conclusion is that, while there are "effectively immutable characteristics"[12] at work in some features of the LGBTQ experience, behavioral choices also play a significant part. The same quite obviously holds true for transgender-related issues: there are active choices involved, and choice is always liable to moral scrutiny and considerations having to do with virtue, character, context, and the good of the whole.

While the "effectively immutable" aspects of homoerotic desire and certain sexual disorientations does provide enough ground to argue not just for tolerance for this population, but that they be received with a spirit of human decency, it does not then render traditional moral standards invalid. Just because a moral teaching or standard is difficult to realize does not mean that it is wrong or that we ought to discard it as a benchmark for society. When a person respectfully and intelligently speaks out against such a radical shift in standards, and he or she is bitterly ridiculed as a "homophobe" or placed in the company of Nazis and Klansmen as a result, a fight certainly begins to feel necessary. In the third installation of his series of articles, speaking of the moral position that many Christians and conservatives find themselves in when confronted with LGBTQ agendas, McLaughlin makes a very useful distinction between sin and scandal. He writes,

> Christ calls us to mercy towards sinners, in recognition that we are all sinners. But it is not hypocritical for sinners to profess virtue and denounce sin; *it is precisely what the Gospel demands of us,* sinners though we are. What Jesus denounces as hypocritical and

11. McLaughlin, "Gays and Christians Part 1," para. 40.
12. McLaughlin, "Gays and Christians Part 1," para. 41.

cowardly is the opposite—pridefully refusing to admit sin and portraying sin as virtue, which causes others to be led astray when they emulate its example. That is implicit in Luke 18:9–14, where Jesus notes that the tax collector who beats his breast in remorse and begs God's mercy goes home justified, while the Pharisee who proclaims his own virtue does not.[13]

In the end, the existence of sin is not the scandal. Rather, it is the requirement that all people should celebrate it. If LGBTQ arguments were centered around conduct, one might see room for differences of opinion about how people should mind their p's and q's. Instead, they shape their arguments around identity, so that disagreement becomes not just a dispute about conduct, but a criticism penetrating to what is perceived to be the very core of that person.[14] The one who disagrees, then, is little more than a bigot or a really nasty individual, perhaps even a Nazi. It is a safe place to hide. Not only does it reduce human identity to mere desires and sexual passions or confusions, but it also too often refuses to admit that other forms of identity might clash with it, and that these other identities must in the very least also be allowed existence if we are to claim a love for liberty.

---

13. McLaughlin, "Gays and Christians Part III," para. 12. Emphasis in the original.

14. I have made a distinction above between identity and person, a distinction that I will further clarify in the sequel to this work, *The Transfiguration of Nature*. In sum, from a theological perspective, identity is subject to, and indeed arises out of, conditions, time, and mutability. Identity is something we acquire and construct through our experiences, memories, expectations, conditioning, formed opinions, and so on. Personhood, on the other hand, while utterly unique to each individual, is rooted in the absolute, unconditioned freedom and unity of God, as it has participation in God. It is a given, not something we can choose or construct. It is that aspect of ourselves that we might say is created in God's image (Gen 1:26–27) as opposed to the aspect of ourselves created in the likeness, say, of the sinful parent (Gen 5:1–3). Both are necessary to human life, but identity without personhood is a monstrous reduction of human dignity, for not only are identities necessarily confining, but they are also subject to confusion and corruption. It is this very Christian understanding of human personhood that has laid the groundwork for democratic society in the first place. Losing sight of God, however, we have lost sight of personhood, and so are left only with identities. Hence, we have become embroiled in a battle for the amplification of personalities that serves only in the end to reduce persons to mere orientations, a sure path to spiritual slavery. Not only this, but it causes social bedlam. Incarcerating our personhood in identities that we mistake for absolutes drives us to amplify private predilections in a futile attempt at gaining freedom. It is a catch-22, for the more we amplify identities to try to free them, the more enslaved to identities we become. True freedom is in being persons, embedded in God, and so in his whole creation, where slavery to identity is overcome by its partaking of God's unconditioned life, the only true liberty. Person and identity are not the same thing; they can at times be in conflict.

For the sake of the liberal idea of equality, LGBTQ advocates seem all too willing to deny or to destroy actual differences that exist in the real world. Its effects are exactly the same as the effects of globalization, the promotion and promulgation of Western commercial paradigms the world over that effectively stamps out local cultures, economies, and the communal relationships and landscapes that sustain them. This kind of tactic, however effective in securing the desired results, cannot go arm in arm with a conservationist's plea to protect local cultures and the lands that have formed them, nor even can it partner with an honest commitment to diversity. Nevertheless, these arguments tend to keep us locked in relativistic, atomistic patterns of thinking, for while they account for the promotion of individual differences, they still do not take up the question of obligation. How does personal conduct influence culture, and how does culture in turn use and shape the land?

A more traditional understanding of the human being asserts our embeddedness within a vast universe of givens. This embeddedness charges the human life with moral and ethical significance, which compels us to realize greater capacities than merely being a swirling mass of caprices. The moral imperative, of which the desire for liberty and equality is certainly an example, sets us apart from other creatures. While driving us to ask the question of liberty and equality, that imperative also requires us to discern between those things that should be healthily amplified and encouraged and those that should not. The moral imperative runs much deeper than presumptuously trying to prove our liberality by accepting with a smile and no small amount of intellectual laziness whatever bizarre monstrosity presents itself, or taking up the cause of anyone who deems him- or herself a victim. Moral discernment requires us to inquire into the nature of the monstrosity or the cause, to test the spirits. An environmentalist would certainly take a conservative stance against spraying a chemical on a field without knowing the nature and properties of that chemical and its effects, both proven and potential, on the integrity of the land. Why would we not take the same approach when confronted with social pressure groups and the worldviews they wish to promulgate? Not all worldviews, not all ideas, are equal. A man marrying a man is ontologically a wholly different thing than a woman marrying a man. Men and women are not the same. To deny their difference is to be a denier of science on a wholly grander scale than those who might argue against global warming, for an example. Indeed, there cannot be a husband without a wife, nor a wife without a husband, as there cannot be hot without cold, dry without wet, day without night. The one gives definition to the other. The relationship between these poles is complimentary, not equal. The one gives the other its existence and demarcation. Without the one, the other disappears. This is what it means to have a life embedded within a vast amount of givens; we do not get to make it all up. If we do, that is all we will be doing: dwelling in an ungrounded fantasy.

Certainly, the moral imperative runs deeper than the standard of personal gratification or the amplification of individual preferences and desire. The gardener must make choices given the whole of the garden, and the farmer, too, given the whole of his farm, as well as the conservationist given the whole of the land. Human culture finds its ground in these decisions, but it also finds its ground in the agriculture of the heart, in the culling of the noxious weeds that grow within us that threaten to choke out a greater potential, to quell a greater life, or to obscure a deeper identity. Human intuition has realized that we hold a unique place among all creatures—by design, by evolution, or by some combination of the two, it matters not. The very fact that we conceive of ourselves as human or can imperil our planet proves this to be so. This is not justification for snubbing our embeddedness in the givens; it only means that, like all the other distinct creatures, we humans shoulder our own genius.

This unique place, called "dominion" in the Genesis narrative, necessitates obligation, which means that we must discern between health and dereliction. The genius of the Genesis narrative is that, while it is realistic about human dominion (language pointing to a royal task within the order of creation), it is by the very same assertion being realistic about the great evil that humanity is capable of achieving within the created order. The proper exercise of dominion clearly must take place within larger contexts, of the whole order of creation and under the tutelage of divine law and love. These contexts serve as the basis of ethical and moral deliberation; without them, there are no ethics. We do not choose these contexts; we are asked to accept, obey, and work with them on no other grounds than good faith. If we are kings and queens who have dominion, we are also servants, bound to reverential obedience and tribute. In reverence lies our only hope. In obedience lies our happiness and our good. In paying tribute lies the assurance of the earth, at least for our race upon it for the fullness of the allotted time. I hear so much uppity talk among environmentalists about the need to create a new society, to forge a brave new world, and so on, all of which is plainly a mere regurgitation of the consumerist myth of progress. The real task at hand seems rather to stop creating new things and to return to what is—to be stewards, not innovators; participants, not heroes. When the human being dishonors this obedience to what is, when the human being seeks to co-opt God the only Creator and become gods and creators unto ourselves, then the order of nature is disrupted, corrupted, and broken. This embeddedness and the ruin we beget when we fail to honor it is the message of Genesis; a message coupled, that is, with the greater message of the love of God, which continues faithfully and which works to transfigure even in the face of our evil and rebellion. God's fidelity is, as it were, an overflowing fecundity that calls forth from the mass of human evil some good, as a flower from a heap of dung.

The reader may not be comfortable with the religious language that I have invoked here. The moral underpinning, however, is clear: though we possess the power to do great damage, the life that would be good, sane, and not suicidal requires that we do differently. It requires that we comport ourselves with the joyful restraint of humble love and with reverential awe toward the mystery of our embeddedness in nature. But not just this. It requires that we make distinctions based on a true intimacy and reciprocity with the contexts that we inhabit. Having loosened our grip on self-centered reasoning, then we might calmly discern, and take the best courses of action that we can in our discernment.

Our desire to amplify individual choices over communal and natural limitations demonstrates a failure of vision. It reveals that we are not honoring the significance, meaning, and value embedded in the things that lie outside of our own choosing. Our technologies and the uses to which we put them, combined with the underlying assumptions of the free market, have made it easier for us to maintain the illusion that realizing our every caprice is possible, even admirable. When we live according to this aim, however, we strip the world of intrinsic value, even as we deny our embeddedness in the world. In the end, we mostly disfigure ourselves because, so far as we live according to such false or unsustainable objectives, we have removed ourselves from reality. All is not up for grabs; this is not a computer-generated world that we live in, but an actual one. The world cannot bear the imposition of our every whim; not everything is to be manipulated to our ends and profited upon. Environmental degradation, the sicknesses of the land and its increasing inability in many places to support diverse forms of life, prove this to be true. We cannot photoshop the world to make it what we wish it were or desire it to be, nor can we photoshop it into health.

The land is not virtual; it is veritable and valid. That is to say, the world is real; we do not choose it. But we can choose how we will live with it and on it, how we will use it, how we will govern ourselves and all creatures to be prosperous and happy given the realities that it imposes on us and our own limitations in creating perfect utopias. If the body of the earth presents us with a given reality, so do our own bodies. We are bound to acknowledge as part of the context of nature and bodily existence the dual gender traits of man and woman and the need for both in almost every complex form of life to reproduce and to be fruitful. If this is bigotry, if this is some kind of sinister hegemony, blame nature, not me. However diverse and dissonant its voices may be, LGBTQ thinking very often forwards ideological programs that rival the most pernicious creation-denying philosophies forwarded by mankind, representing a concerted effort to disavow, violate, and annihilate natural bounds. Such ideologies represent a clear expression of our disaffection from, and disfiguration of, nature. Right relationship with the body of the earth begins with our own flesh and blood.

More than this, LGBTQ political victories are fast proving the general theory of revolutions: the oppressed becomes the oppressor. LGBTQ political and social tactics, while effective, alienate and inspire a highly defensive posture in constituencies that environmentalists need to reach the most. We can thank these tactics, in part, for Donald Trump's shocking ascendency. Such people will never vote for the environment, simply because they will never vote for their own cultural and religious demise. Just as the family farmer is expected to get on board or to get squashed by big agriculture's train of progress, so the one who wishes to remain faithful to his tradition is asked to comply or die to this new social evolution (hardly a sustainable one as far as nature is concerned). On the other hand, certain breeds of Christian conservatives sometimes act as if marriage, as central as it is to the full Christian theological vision of redemption, were the only tenet on which the gospel stood. Homosexuality and gender confusion is not the only sin, and certainly not the worst. Would that Christians were at least as equally scandalized by forced participation in the military industrial complex and corporate hegemony with their attendant cultures of earthly might, greed, avariciousness, exploitation, and violence. The early Christians were martyred for taking such stands, and it was their courage and witness to faithful and peaceful love that eventually and astoundingly transformed Roman culture into Christian culture. Who can respect a Christian who runs about busily propping up Donald Trump, a person so evidently untouched by the gospel? I understand the feeling that, if certain issues are lost, all is lost, and the tactics of the Left provide no comfort in this regard and certainly require a bold stand. Still, the gospel cannot be parsed into singular issues. If Christians are to witness to it, their witness must be broader and fuller. They may even find allies where they thought were only enemies.

THE MOVEMENTS AND THEIR UNDERPINNINGS

According to Will Roscoe, who edited a collection of the writings of Harry Hay in the 1950s, Hay first articulated the sentiment that "Lesbians and gay men differ from heterosexuals much as African-Americans, Latinos, Japanese-Americans, and other ethnic groups differ from Euro-Americans." He urged homosexuals to overcome their self-hatred and their shame and take pride in their "lovely sexuality." Around the same time, the equivalent idea was expressed by Donald Webster Cory in *The Homosexual in America*:

> We who are homosexual are a minority, not only numerically, but also as a result of a caste-like status in society . . . Our minority status is similar, in a variety of respects, to that of national, religious, and other ethnic groups: in the denial of civil liberties; in the legal, extra-legal, and quasi-legal discrimination; in the assignment of an inferior social position; in the exclusion from the mainstream of life and culture.[15]

Norman Podhoretz, a writer for Commentary Magazine who traces the success of the gay rights movement in an article entitled "How the Gay-Rights Movement Won" asserts that "In those days very few people, whether gay or straight, were prepared to see homosexuality as comparable to race or ethnicity."[16]

At a later time, gay activists began to draw on the successes of the civil rights movement, which prepared a greater number of people to consider with some seriousness Hay and Cory's claims. Such claims were, in fact, borrowed directly from the ideas that had been and would continue to shape the struggle for equal rights for minorities, especially black people, a struggle so long overdue. Inspired by these labors, gay rights groups began staging boisterous and confrontational demonstrations against target

---

15. Cory, *Homosexual in America*, 3, 13–14.
16. Podhoretz, "Gay-Rights Movement," para. 22.

institutions, notably the enforcers and composers of law, educational institutions, various medical and psychiatric associations, and religious communities. For instance, Mark Mondimore, a psychiatrist, in his 1996 work *A Natural History of Homosexuality*, recounts the following:

> Emboldened by their successes in opposing police harassment, gay-liberation activists turned their attention to another historical opponent: the psychiatric profession. In 1970, gay activists stormed the annual meeting of the American Psychiatric Association, confronted psychoanalyst Irving Bieber during a panel discussion on homosexuality, and called him a "motherfucker" in front of his shocked colleagues.[17]

The APA responded as the universities had: it capitulated. Within three years, homosexuality was removed from the APA's *Diagnostic and Statistical Manual* as a listed mental disorder. The American Psychological Association and the National Association of Social Workers followed suit. Though it was claimed that these changes were based on scientific research, it is clear that scientific research played a minimal part in the decisions. The deciding factors were due to political and social pressure. Podhoretz explains that much of the scientific "evidence" cited to back the changes were

> compiled by Alfred Kinsey, and yet when his estimate of the incidence of male homosexuality (10 percent) would later be exposed as wildly overblown by a much more rigorous study conducted by the National Opinion Research Center at the University of Chicago (which arrived at a figure of 2.6 percent), and by the even more definitive Sex in America (2.8 percent), the APA would make no move to reverse itself again.[18]

McLaughlin is softer in his appraisal of this stage of LGBTQ activism, one reason why he himself was sympathetic to the cause. He states that,

> Early LGBT-rights arguments from the 1960s to the 1980s were often framed in terms of liberty, most prominently the fight against sodomy laws and the obvious injustice, highlighted in the years of the AIDS crisis, of gay couples being denied hospital visitation rights enjoyed even by unmarried opposite-sex domestic

---

17. Mondimore, *Natural History of Homosexuality*, 239.

18. Podhoretz, "Gay-Rights Movement," para. 25. A study conducted on the exit poll of the 1992 November election revealed even smaller numbers, 1 percent. See Tingle, "Ideology and Politics of the Gay Movement," sec. "Accuracy of the Ideology of the Gay Movement."

partners. Some social conservative hardliners, of course, were unsympathetic even to these arguments, but for many of us, there was a strong case for recognizing gay liberty to form intimate associations and for passing laws to create space for those liberties.[19]

His estimate of the marriage debate changes in tone. He reflects:

> But from the very outset of the same-sex marriage debate, LGBT activists chose to pursue a maximalist litigation strategy deliberately modeled on the civil rights movement's drive to destroy Jim Crow. This strategy by its nature de-emphasized liberty and mutual tolerance in favor of a winner-take-all battle for control of the law.[20]

In order for this model to be successful, it required the suppression of any distinction between behavior and identity. The strategy was also convenient for circumventing American voters:

> Given the political terrain from the early 1990s through the mid-2000s, this [strategy] was a coldly rational calculation . . . because public opinion at large strongly opposed recognizing same-sex marriages, while the legal profession and thus the courts was mostly in favor, so the best results were likely to come from appealing to lawyers while freezing out voters.[21]

According to McLaughlin, popular opinion favored traditional marriage as late as 2008. In that same year, Barack Obama and Hilary Clinton both campaigned on marriage platforms that opposed same-sex unions. Obama did not change his tune until 2012. Clinton followed suit a year later.

In the early days of the movement, homosexuals chided leery people by stating that the source of their mistrust was their own repressed homoerotic feelings. Anyone was in danger of becoming a homosexual, everyone had such feelings, and some—the brave ones—choose to openly express them. This rhetoric changed drastically after the submission of the medical and psychiatric associations. If homosexuality is not a sickness, if it is not a psychological idiosyncrasy, if it is not a choice that could be morally scrutinized like all choices, then it is inborn. It is not a choice at all, and if not a choice or an aberration then it is totally out of reach of any moral

---

19. McLaughlin, "Gays and Christians Part III," para. 28.
20. McLaughlin, "Gays and Christians Part III," para. 31.
21. McLaughlin, "Gays and Christians Part III," para. 33.

consideration. To repress it is to repress the very nature of a person, as God created that person to be. Since that time, the movement has worked diligently to change the popular jargon about sexuality from "sexual preference" to "sexual orientation." Young people today will not remember the time when "sexual preference" was the politically correct term. The reality of homoerotic feelings notwithstanding, in this line of reasoning, the will plays no part in behavior. Might we just as easily say that a racist, a pedophile, a zoophile, a "rageaholic" who consistently abuses women, someone who is depressed, or a greedy businessman are the way they are because they were merely born in this manner, as God created and intended them to be? It would be a digression to get into a discussion here about the difference between the God-given potential for the human nature and the actual current state of human life given the realities of sin and free will. Suffice it to say that, if God intends for the chronically depressed and the chronically abusive to be this way, or if he intends that people lay waste to and poison his creation in their avaricious pride, it is no wonder that we find it so easy to be hostile toward God! I would not find such a God worthy of worship if God were so.

As much as circumstance shapes our lives, and as much as life is largely about dealing with what we have been dealt, such rhetoric is not entirely acceptable for anyone who believes in a modicum of personal responsibility. Even people with developmental disabilities, while one may not expect such a person to become a math professor, have shown themselves capable of growth and self-mastery with patient nurture, as opposed to impatient or discounting indulgence. If we do not believe in personal responsibility, then there can be no environmentalism at all. Instead, we must resign ourselves to being a society of victims, celebrating our brokenness and our passions until some great implosion wipes us out forever. A gay activist handbook proposes this very strategy. It instructs,

> First, the mainstream should be told that gays are victims of fate, in the sense that most never had a choice to accept or reject their sexual preference. The message must read: "As far as gays can tell, they were born gay, just as you were born heterosexual or white or black or bright or athletic. Nobody ever tricked or seduced them; they never made a choice, and are not morally blameworthy. What they do isn't willfully contrary—it's only natural for them. This twist of fate could as easily have happened to you!"[22]

22. Kirk and Madsen, "Overhauling of Straight America," para. 10. This essay was expanded into a book and published in 1990 as *After the Ball: How America Will Conquer*

Another advantage comes from declaring homosexuality as inborn. Gay propaganda and gay education could no longer be seen as a threat to children; it would only assist those who were born gay to reconcile themselves to this fact with less trauma, while those born heterosexual would not be affected. Though scientific evidence for the much sought-after "gay gene" continues to be scanty, a wave of liberation followed in the wake of this strategy. Gay magazines and advocates sung the praises of the pleasures of gay sex, and the promiscuity that was invariably associated with the lifestyle was hailed as superior to the routine, fainthearted, lackluster sex practiced by middle-class monogamous couples. It plainly felt good to be gay. Those of us who came of age in the eighties do not need to be reminded of the dark side of this party.

Randy Shilts, author of the most authoritative book on the AIDS epidemic, *And the Band Played On*, who would also die of the disease, gives an account of the situation before the epidemic broke. Gay men, he reported,

> were being washed by tide after tide of increasingly serious infections. First it was syphilis and gonorrhea. Gay men made up about 80 percent of the 70,000 annual patients to [San Francisco's] VD clinics. Easy treatment had imbued them with such a cavalier attitude toward venereal diseases that many gay men saved their waiting-line numbers, like little tokens of desirability, and the clinic was considered an easy place to pick up both a shot and a date.[23]

Podhoretz rounds out the picture:

> None of this deterred a gay paper from running an article in praise of "rimming" (oral-anal sex) as a "revolutionary act." Along the same lines, Edmund White, the co-author of *The Joy of Gay Sex*, even proposed at a public meeting that "gay men should wear their sexually transmitted diseases like red badges of courage in a war against a sex-negative society." A young homosexual named

---

its *Fear and Hatred of Gays in the 1990s*. A 2015 interview with Hunter Madsen gives his own account of this work: Cleary, "Hunter Madsen and the Homosexual Agenda." For some reason hard to identify except as being solely for polemical purposes, the interview begins by equating the alarm and concern that Madsen's document has inspired among certain groups with alarm and concern inspired by a document designed to stir up anti-Semitic sentiment that was verified a hoax. The interview makes it very clear that the "overhauling of straight America" is anything but a hoax. It was written with serious intentions, and it has been influential. As such, why would it not be highly discussed and debated, especially by those people and groups whom it seeks to shame and silence?

23. Shilts, *And the Band Played On*, 39.

Michael Callen, who was present at that meeting, who had already had three thousand sexual partners, and who (like White himself) would eventually come down with AIDS, remembered thinking: "Every time I get the clap I'm striking a blow for the sexual revolution."[24]

How is treating one's own body and the bodies of others in such a manner different from misusing the earth? Both are done in the name of pleasure, liberty from tradition, and the attendant idea of progress.

The revelry was taken to the streets in the annual pride parades, often designed to offend. The Sisters of Perpetual Indulgence, an activist group of gay men who dress like nuns in speedos, are one such example, along with the hunky Jesus competition held in San Francisco. One has to wonder why public displays such as these, so clearly aimed with hostility at a certain constituency, are deemed to be okay while it is not okay for a baker to quietly refuse to provide a cake for a same-sex marriage on the grounds of a religious conviction.[25] Who is bigoted? The Sisters of Perpetual Indulgence, as a part of their activism, were also known to disrupt church services, defile things that were considered by some groups to be sacred, and to stand in communion lines in their inflammatory outfits. What did the churches do? Many followed the way of the universities and the associations; they caved.

AIDS did not immediately slow the party. Podhoretz points out that, "On the contrary, these acts were now represented as perfectly proper so long as they were practiced 'safely' (i.e., with a condom or a dental dam). And most incredible of all, children in the early grades of primary school were even given lessons in the correct techniques."[26]

Despite the continuing revelry among many, the public faces of LGBTQ movements have cooled recently. Going after the redefinition, not only of marriage but also of family (and that is what the issue is about; it is not about the right to marry, but about the legal definition of what the right of marriage is), some gay literature has tended to play down the promiscuity, comforting the mainstream that this is not representative. Most gay people, we are told, value the same things that most heterosexuals value,

---

24. Podhoretz, "Gay-Rights Movement," para. 35. Three thousand sexual partners? One a day every day for over eight years. Can this be so?

25. "Court Rules Bakery Illegally Discriminated Against Gay Couple." Lawsuits such as this are not uncommon.

26. Podhoretz, "Gay-Rights Movement," para. 40.

such as a settled family life. Upon social acceptance, the radical aspects of the movement will disappear. Daniel Mendelsohn, a writer for New York magazine, hopes that this is not the case. Lamenting this new line of rhetoric, he calls it the "heterosexualization of gay culture." He is concerned that gay people are "less likely to celebrate the initiation into the world of avid sexuality . . . than they are to emphasize the importance (who knew?) of family ties."[27] Two things are happening here. For one, it may very well be the case that some gay people are getting tired of constant instability. They sense that, despite all of the fun and excitement of the lifestyle, there is a profound human experience that they are squandering. This direction is promising. Secondly, the architects of this movement recognize that, once marriage and family as traditionally understood in nearly all cultures and all times are redefined to normalize same-sex relations, the lifestyle itself will be fully justified, totally unchallenged and unchallengeable; secured in perpetuity. The same gay PR manual quoted above confirms this latter tactic. Gay publicity should leave the average person with no excuses to say, "they are not like us." Public campaigns for gays should feature persons who are depicted in every way to be decent, "upright, appealing and admirable by straight standards, . . . indistinguishable from the straights" that these campaigns are trying to reach. "Only under such conditions will the message be read correctly: 'These folks are victims of a fate that could have happened to me.'"[28]

Then, the manual barks the final orders:

> At a later stage of the media campaign for gay rights—long after other gay ads have become commonplace—it will be time to get tough with remaining opponents. To be blunt, they must be vilified . . . Our goal here is twofold. First, we seek to replace the mainstream's self-righteous pride about its homophobia with shame and guilt. Second, we intend to make the antigays look so nasty that average Americans will want to dissociate themselves from such types.[29]

So much for tolerance. Here is an expression of a totalistic objective. Must we wonder why this movement disgusts so many? Originally starting as an appeal for tolerance, we now have what may be counted among the most intolerant movements to gain a footing in this country. There will not

---

27. Mendelsohn, "We're Here, We're Queer," 27.
28. Kirk and Madsen, "Overhauling Straight America," 11.
29. Kirk and Madsen, "Overhauling Straight America," 20.

be burnings or lynching, but there will be trial after trial, witch hunt after witch hunt, as the LGBTQ crusaders exact the vengeance that they think they deserve from their straw men. It will be one of the most religiously intolerant wielders of power, all in the warm and fuzzy name of "nondiscrimination" and equal rights for all. The Dalai Lama has semi-courageously admitted that, according to the Buddhist precepts, homosexual behavior is forbidden. In his usual relativism, he declares it wrong for Buddhists but not for society.[30] One wonders why something that would hinder an individual from reaching sanity and the state of blessedness should be okay for a whole society to practice, but whatever! Conservative Jews and Christians, as well as most Muslims, also feel that it is an improper and unnatural use of our bodies, of the good gift of sexuality. These groups will be the targets of the shame tactics of the gay propagandist. Though there are LGBTQ people who identify with the American conservatives (so-called), it is the liberal Left that has championed the cause and chaperoned it through the halls of society, arm in arm with the environmental cause. This is the reason why we write all of this, and we will turn to the examination of this close relationship presently.

CORE PRINCIPALS OF THE MOVEMENTS AND THEIR CONGRUENCY WITH CONSERVATIONIST AIMS

The LGBTQ constituency appears to us as a monolithic lobby seeking a unified end. Nevertheless, as we would expect from human beings—and especially from a group of human beings so hypersensitized to domination and oppression—it is peppered with its own history of internal conflicts, as has already been stated above. Notably, there is internal division around the issue of marriage. Some perceive the hard-won right to gay marriage to be a concession of what the pages of homosexual literature has historically characterized as an oppressive, patriarchal institution founded on possession and power. For these people, sadly, the possibility that lifelong, monogamous relationships might fulfill a deep human longing for intimacy, heroic love, self-gifting, and participation in a life larger than one's own seems beyond the pale of the imagination. To be sure, those who wed consumerism and sex, as the consumers of sexual encounter do, will never be inspired by

---

30. Lattin, "Dali Lama Speaks on Gay Sex."

the virtue of fidelity. Nor is it considered that the discipline of stable commitments not only lends integrity to intimate and familial relationships, but helps bolster honest business relationships and the integrity of other interpersonal, communal interactions as well. It also undergirds a strong conservationist ethic. In keeping with the movement's push to re-define reality, not only sexually but socially, some LGBTQ thinkers desire to do away with institutions such as marriage altogether, creating instead their own "networks of accountability" that will lead to further liberation from the oppressive assumptions of "heteronormativity."[31] In some ways, it may be better that they do this, rather than insisting that we all mechanically and uncritically celebrate their lifestyles and identities while throwing our own into the garbage.

The issue of homosexual marriage is thorny. For one, like most of the shallow debates of our time, it is conceived of as solely a matter of rights without even a well-rounded reflection on the nature of rights themselves. To talk about rights, however, is already to obscure the real issue at stake. No one wants to deny anyone the right to legal marriage. What conservative-minded people wish to spend more time discussing is which definition of legal marriage best serves human society, and best honors nature, in the long run. Should marriage be conceived of as a private contract between two isolated individuals? Does marriage have its base merely in the self-contained, sentimental choices and desires of atomized people? Or, is marriage also a union that undergirds a strong, stable society and connects that society not only to the past, to the men and women of our family trees, but also to the future through the rearing of children? If society is to bless a marriage, how does each marriage bless society and further its common goals? A US Supreme Court ruling against bigamy in 1878 described marriage in the following terms:

> Marriage, while from its very nature a sacred obligation, is nevertheless, in most civilized nations, a civil contract, and usually regulated by law. Upon it society may be said to be built, and out of its fruits spring social relations and social obligations and duties, with which government is necessarily required to deal.[32]

The public did not perceive this ruling as denying anyone the right to marry. Rather, the ruling only reinforced the legal definition of the

---

31. Jessica Max Stein of Make/Shift Magazine quoted on the webpage "Against Equality," para. 4.

32. See Reynolds v. the U.S.

institution as comprising the union of one man and one woman within a definite social context, a bond itself bound up in social obligations. Marriage, as far as the law is concerned, is not a purely private affair. The law requires a license to marry. If I applied to marry my sister, I would be denied—not denied the right to marry, only denied my sister for a bride, just as the ruling cited above did not deny Mr. Reynolds of a bride, but only of having two of them.

LGBTQ literature and commentary, in keeping with the liberal extremism that inspires it, has decried most social institutions, believing things traditional to be repressive and backwards. It is no surprise that it should also disdain marriage, as it has generally done from the start, and so seek to redefine it more on its own terms. It seems to me that allowing homosexual couples to enjoy the legal allowances of marriage, such as shared health insurance and Social Security benefits, does not present a problem per se. Redefining legal marriage as something other than the union of a man and a woman for the sake of rearing the next generation of citizens, however, requires further deliberation. So, too, does the rash belief that a child does not need a mother and a father, though perhaps two daddies are better than no parents at all. Then there is also the question of technically assisted reproduction, the only reproductive option available to monogamous homosexual couples, a question that moves beyond a discussion of homosexual marriage, for it affects heterosexual couples as well. While so many women are aborting their children, others are taking fertility pills and making trips to the sperm bank, choosing the genetic characteristics they would like in their child, as if shopping. What do these practices imply, not only about how we view our children, but also about how we view and understand our humanity and how we appreciate or depreciate the linkages of that humanity with the processes, limitations, and structures of nature? Are children merely commodities that we can manufacture and consume at will, choosing them off a shelf or discarding them at our whim? If a conservationist decries certain uses of technologies to control and manipulate and perhaps even disrupt, degrade, or devalue natural processes and cycles central to the land's integrity, fertility, and heath, is it then okay to do this with our own bodies, our own fertility, and our own children? Are we not also a part of nature and members of the world ecosystem?

In any case, if for no other reason than out of a respect for real diversity and religious liberty, let us at least agree to disagree. If a priest or a rabbi, for example, tells a same-sex couple that he or she cannot marry them, so be it. The same holds true for an adoption agency that, due especially to religious considerations, believes a child's best interest is in being reared by a committed heterosexual couple. Or, for that matter, a photographer who, because of religious conviction, does not want to take photos at a same-sex marriage. Accept the no and move on; stop the witch-hunts and legal burnings. Unfortunately, we have already heard the objective of the movement: "we intend to make the antigays look so nasty that average Americans will want to dissociate themselves from such types."[33] On the other hand, allowing gay marriage on a civil level could just as well be seen as a small victory for the institution, as it represents at least a willingness to concede, on the part of some homosexuals (and to the chagrin of others), that life-long monogamous commitments and stable households are essentially good and worthy institutions. More than this, they fulfill deep-seated human longings for heroic love, stability, and the opportunity for profound intimacy with partner and place. Unless, of course, the motive is merely to defile and undermine these values, and to mock them. Time will tell.

In the end, what we see here are movements undergirded not only by sexual consumerism, but also by the laissez-faire attitudes of modernist liberalism, this time as it relates to sexual behavior and ages-old human institutions that, despite the propaganda, are not dogmatic and political in essence, but organic and communal. Somewhat shockingly, there is a tendency within these movements to aim the liberal idea of progress—that is, the throwing-off of the perceived hindrances of tradition and the past—toward gender itself, suggesting that these movements' hostilities are ultimately directed toward the very order of nature. From its beginnings as an organized social and political force first comprised of gays and lesbians, LGBTQ populations have consistently set their sights on undermining not only organic human institutions such as marriage, but also on undermining religious commitments, educational institutions, and medical insights, to name but a few. They overindulge when they refuse to stop there, and when they seek further to defy and redefine the realities of natural sexual characteristics. How sad to disparage normative heterosexual behavior as oppressive, and heterosexuals themselves as little more than a political elite who desire to maintain some repressive tradition—that is, love between a man and a woman—and impose it on an otherwise asexual world, as if we and the rest of mammalian life were little more than so many amoebas. This is not to deny that gender asymmetries exist, and that some people

---

33. Kirk and Madsen, "Overhauling Straight America," 20.

have these crosses to carry. In fact, biologists are finding an increasing occurrence of these asymmetries in certain organisms, such as amphibians, cueing them off to environmental degradation because these organisms act as the proverbial canaries in the mine when it comes to pollution. Scientists have directly linked these gender asymmetries to various toxins in the environment, such as chemicals found in certain plastics, pesticides, and herbicides; an increased amount of estrogen in the water correlated with the use of birth control products; and possibly growth hormones in the food stream.[34] The sustained ingestion of hormonal birth-control products on the part of mothers may also cause hormonal imbalances and problems in their children.[35] I am not suggesting that all LGBTQ characteristics can be linked to these kinds of causes, but we would be irresponsible to not take into account this troubling evidence for the love of our society, human health, and the health of the land. Whatever the causes are, we must affirm that when such conditions present themselves in humans, those who bear them should not be ostracized or subjugated. Nevertheless, accepting gender irregularities on the one hand, and the mutinous celebration of throwing off what are scorned as the repressive confines of gender norms on the other, are two very different things. The Greater London Council Women's Committee argued in its 1986 publication *Tracking Heterosexism: A Handbook of Lesbian Rights* that "it has become clear that heterosexuality, like the assumed superiority of men, is not natural but acquired. The fact that the majority of men and women may choose [heterosexuality] as their preferred form of sexuality has more to do with persuasion, coercion and threat of ostracism than with its superiority as a form of sexuality."[36]

Shockingly, the rhetoric goes as far as to claim that normative gender characteristics, built into the very fabric of nature, are sinister and repressive choices when we are to believe that homosexuals themselves have no choice! Such language is downright abusive; we might call it "homosexist" or "heterophobic." Is male and female now a captivity that must be overcome for the sake of some tyrannical ideology of liberty and freedom? Or, is it for the sake of an insatiable greed for certain sexual escapades and gratifications? Perhaps we attack the twofold nature of gender out of a genuine

34. See, for example, Zimmer, "Unraveling the Mystery."

35. See, for example, Migeon, "Birth Control Pill."

36. Quoted in Tingle, "Ideology and Politics of Gay Movement," 30. WorldCat lists *Tracking Heterosexism* at http://www.worldcat.org/title/tackling-heterosexism-a-handbook-of-lesbian-rights/oclc/52920816.

disaffection from, and hatred of, nature and civilization itself. To return to the fourth core belief of the anti-environmental group, the "wise use" movement (cited at the beginning of this chapter), we must wonder whether the belief that "our limitless imaginations can break through natural limits to make earthly goods and carrying capacity virtually limitless" is at all wise, at all possible, or if it is plainly megalomaniacal lunacy. As we throw off restraints and moral principles that would guide and limit the uses and abuses of markets and technologies, as we throw off restraints to justify an unhindered and much celebrated rape of the earth and its resources, of traditional cultures and the local economies that support them, now we argue for the overthrow even of gender restraints. Can such a strange cry as this ever undergird or even sit side by side with a serious-minded call to the world to regulate our activities through a moral and ethical regard for the limitations of nature and the value of traditional cultures and ecosystems? Can this poison rhetoric, so condescending of normative human relationships and loves, ever inspire people to limit themselves for the good of the whole, including the good of the body of the earth? Would a doctrine of promiscuity and sexual exploitation inspire a person to respect the land's virginity in places set aside as untouched wilderness? Could a practice of sexual consumerism and adventure undergird the conservationist's plea for local commitments, a plea to remain in and care for a place? Such a plea is necessary, not only to limit the wastes and pollution of travel and mobility and the damage of globalism, but also to foster the necessary intimacy with land and neighbor that would make for true community and love for the earth.

I remember hiking in the Rocky Mountains one fine late-summer evening. In a cool wooded grove at the edge of a browning meadow, I happened upon a large herd of elk. Their contentment was brimming over as they happily chewed their cuds and lazed about on the pine-needle softened forest floor. I recognized the dominant male right away. He was massive, his head and brawny antlers towering above the heads of the rest. Quietly inching my way toward the reclining herd, I was able to get quite close to them, almost sidling in among them. When I edged in a little too closely, the bull rose to his feet, enquiringly sniffing at the air. Immediately, all the other elk took the cue. They, too, rose to their feet, and were now nervously peering about. I remained motionless for what seemed an eternity, until finally the bull relaxed again, dropping to his haunches and tranquilly resuming his repose. All the other elk did the same. Poor creatures; perhaps someone ought to tell them that they are all oppressed. I suppose they would not listen, anyhow.

LGBTQ movements, especially in their most extreme articulations, have distracted and undermined the conservationist cause. Their arguments tend toward the academic, and are fixated on a minority special interest. Yet, these movements have consumed so much of our public money, time, and attention. As we have seen from their own words, their objectives and their means often border on totalitarian and pernicious. They base themselves on a revisionist history, further a self-absorbed notion of rights without regard to larger imperatives, and disdain organic systems of biology and social order. They laugh at self-regulation and boundaries, and are intolerant of other viewpoints. Most importantly, they have alienated a great number of people who will also now never consider the more urgent issues put on the table alongside theirs, the issues that affect the majority of us the most. Conservationists would do well to distance themselves from movements such as these, and rather to focus their efforts on reaching the people who need to be reached the most, offering to them sound moral and ethical reasons why conservation matters for us all. These moral reasons are based in the fact that we are contingent creatures, dependent on systems, processes, and on a natural order that we do not and cannot choose; reasons which are bigger than our individual predilections and desires, and bigger even than our social, political, and economic orders. The stability and integrity of the latter are, in fact, dependent on the health and vitality of the former. It is time to stop putting our own choices and penchants first; it is time to throw off the adolescent libertarian ideologies that undermine our embrace of and joyful consent to the embeddedness of human life in the glorious confines of nature.

Chapter 6

The Moral Logic of Conservation: Technological Infatuations and Membership with the Land

Once, the governing human metaphor was pastoral or agricultural, and it clarified, and so preserved in human care, the natural cycles of birth, growth, death, and decay. But modern humanity's governing metaphor is that of the machine... By means of the machine metaphor we have eliminated any fear or awe or reverence or humility or delight or joy that might have restrained us in our use of the world. We have indeed learned to act as if our sovereignty were unlimited and as if our intelligence were equal to the universe. Our "success" is a catastrophic demonstration of our failure. The industrial Paradise is a fantasy in the minds of the privileged and the powerful; the reality is a shambles... There is no aspect of our life as a people that is not now under the dominance of this industrial dream of the future-as-Paradise.[1]

—WENDELL BERRY

ONE OF THE MANY linguistic and relational confusions of our time has to do with science and technology. Though one is derived from the other, these are not the same thing. Science, strictly speaking, is in the business of describing not prescribing. Leaving aside for the time being the subjective

1. Berry, *Unsettling of America*, 60–61.

grey zones and biases inherent even in the practice of science, science's quest—at least within the modernist assumptions under which it is currently conducted— is to describe objective fact. As such, it claims a certain moral neutrality and assumes that it goes about its business free of bias and tradition. Again, such a claim is unfounded, since the kind and quality of knowledge that science takes for granted does not take into account all the other ways that human beings come to know the world, nor does it always take into account the limits of human knowledge.[2] For now, we will put these complications aside and simply reaffirm that science is in the business of describing, not prescribing. A biologist, for example, might study and describe the behavior of a certain animal. When she takes that data and then makes a prediction about some kind of evolutionary direction that the animal might take based on her observations, she has left the realm of description and has entered the realm of speculation.

Technology, on the other hand, makes use of scientific description and observation; it puts these to work not only in the human social realm, but also on the landscape. Therefore, technology is not science and cannot claim the same moral neutrality as science. Insofar as technology is an action (putting scientific observation to work), it demands our scrutiny on moral and ethical terms. It is our duty to subject technology to well-considered standards. We always subject technology to standards, but these standards are rarely well-considered or even conscious. Indeed, they are often downright dubious, such as the near-sighted standards of convenience, efficiency, profit, change for the sake of change, doing something because we can, and so forth. As we have been affirming throughout this work, with all freedom comes responsibility, and the greater the freedom the greater the responsibility. Knowledge, too, broadens obligation. Just because something becomes possible in expanded knowledge does not mean that doing it is the best idea. Many things are possible in my life, but only a limited number of actions would be appropriate given the goals and standards I have set for it. Even more to the point, only a limited number of actions would be appropriate because of the relationships that sustain my life. Because I value the intimacy I have forged with my wife, I would not take actions that would undermine the intimacy and trust we have built over time and with some struggle. Because I value the land, I would do all

---

2. Again, I point the reader here to Karl Stern's wonderful epistemological/psychological study *The Flight from Woman*, which documents the rise and dominance in modern times of the rational over and against relational/intuitive/poetic ways of coming to knowledge.

that I can to care for it and not to impose unrealistic demands upon it. The more we recognize these kinds of relationships, the more limited our possibilities in life become. Change and development are not progress unless there is a clear end in mind, and the end is dubious unless it is envisioned within the concrete contexts of our lives. Unless our goals are formulated in a deep consideration of relationships (such as our embeddedness in human and natural ecosystems), and in obligations to concerns larger than our own individual drives, our goals are fallacious because they ignore too much of reality. Ethics is not merely an idea or ideology that we superimpose upon behavior. Sound ethics emerge from relationships and things in themselves. We may tell ourselves that we are simply making a living at something, perhaps through the proliferation of devices and conveniences. When these objectively erode so much of our lives, livelihoods, and land, however, we must ask if this activity will do society well in the long run. Ethical questions emerge from the real effects of our actions in the realm of relationships. No person acts in a vacuum. There is an effect to every action. The disorder of human relationships in families and communities, not to mention the waning capacities of our land, is a sign of a deep moral crisis in our culture.

TECHNOLOGICAL ELITES

Consumerism drives technology, to be sure. We create our destiny either willingly or blindly by what we buy. But technology also shapes what we buy; like all advertising (and much technology is advanced for the sake of making sales), it creates desires and needs where none existed before. It also creates moral dilemmas where none existed before, such as the dilemma of prolonging life by artificial, technological means. Just because it is possible to maintain a person's vital signs by a machine, does that mean that we should do so? Is pulling the proverbial plug the same as murder? Because we now have the ability to prolong a life by technology, would it therefore be murderous if we do not do it, or is it merely surrendering to the natural course of life?

Whether it be evolutionary scientists disdaining certain religious groups, genetic scientists disdaining GMO protestors, or environmentalists disdaining "climate-change deniers," one often hears the charge pressed on certain people that they are "anti-science." Charges such as these are fired across political lines, defying party politics or cultural backgrounds. That the phenomenon defies party politics may be indicative of a larger cause than a mere anti-science attitude among the ranks of a certain political or social camp. Perhaps we are witnessing a pushback, however disorganized and unexamined, against a scientific, technological elite that constantly encroaches on, and often invades, our lives, advancing various programs that we do not always entirely understand or accept. Multiple times a day, billions of people see the Google homepage, where Google is quietly reshaping society in a liturgical fashion. There, those who are in the driver's seat at Google commemorate their own assembly of saints, all of the holy ones of secular society. They choose the holidays they wish to remind us of, and so forth. This is not mere innocent fun; they are shaping the social mind deliberately. Every culture does it, but those who wish to maintain cultural values that do not always run parallel to liberal, secular Western values (advanced globally as if they were universal and absolute) need to, and will, resist efforts like these. This is just an example of how technocrats shape culture deliberately, as they do without conscious deliberation, and why there might be resistance despite the conveniences that their technologies may achieve.

Even without the class- or culture-struggle analogies, most all people would admit that there are deeper questions that must be addressed before various technologies are deployed. Just because we can do something, just because something is possible, does that mean that we should do it or that our doing it is somehow inevitable, as if we were passive victims of the technologies we create? How are potentially good technologies being used to exploit, to maximize the purveyor's benefits at an unacceptable cost to others, and to shape society in dubious ways? Scientific fact may be amoral, but putting science to work is never amoral because it is a human activity. We use our knowledge to ends that are not amoral, and we simply cannot trust certain technologies in the hands of all people. Nuclear energy, for example, promises much. I think it is a viable option for relatively clean energy, especially given the rate that we currently utilize energy and our unwillingness to use less. At the same time, however, the advancement of nuclear power has left us crouching in terror, not only because of the dangers inherent in using it to generate electricity, but because of its potential use for warfare. We have to marvel at the science behind the nuclear age. At the same time, we have to admit that we have opened a veritable Pandora's box into the world, what some may feel is an unwanted discovery, for it may only be a matter of time before this wonderful technology destroys us, and that by our own hands.

Television and media provide another example. Through various forms of media, Americans partake of a steady diet of violence mingled with sex, which represents not only a disfiguration of human life and sexual union, but also by extension a cheapening of all life. Copiously served via television shows; in various musical genres, lyrics, and music videos; in movies; and in video games, we do little reflecting on how such a diet forms lives and shapes culture. We are what we eat. To illustrate, studies have linked video game violence to increased delinquent behaviors in children, along with increased aggression, and a decrease in positive social behaviors.[3] When the next school shooting occurs, why will our public discussions remain gridlocked, fixated on gun control and its attendant rights arguments? Why will the media be silent about its contribution to the problem, and the consumer equally unrepentant about his or her treasured but perverse entertainments? According to 1998 statistics, which I can only guess have significantly increased in our time, by the time an average child finishes elementary school, she will have witnessed some eight thousand murders through her TV alone. When she reaches eighteen years of age, her young mind and heart will have been embossed with some two hundred thousand acts of violence via the same screen.[4] Kudos to those who read this and care enough about their children to throw their televisions out the window. The televisions must be hastily followed by our computers, tablets, and smartphones. Is my saying this anti-science? Not at all. It is merely a word of love for our children, and for the society of which they will one day have custody. Indeed, by expulsing these objects, we may find that we can live with less hassle, expense, and commotion, and no small amount of quiet and pleasure, without many of these technologies. My apologies if this is bad for business. Happy will be the day when knowledge is deployed by wisdom; sound economy, whose provision will be enough, will follow.

Even further than this, I am certain that the privileged lives we lead can tend to keep us in an emotionally immature, regressive state. One study has shown that the "app generation," that is, the generation of youth who depend on apps to solve their problems (anything from getting around town, to writing a narrative, to conducting a relationship) demonstrate a

---

3. "Violence in the Media and Entertainment," https://www.aafp.org/about/policies/all/violence-media.html.

4. Mueller, "What You Need to Know," para. 3.

significant loss of creativity and bravado when it comes to problem-solving and risk-taking in real life situations.[5] Other studies have tied the use of various technologies to a rising incidence of child obesity and diabetes; delays in normal development, especially literacy; increases in mental illness and behavior disorders; and a decreased ability to self-regulate and for attentiveness. According to the report, "Diagnoses of ADHD, autism, coordination disorder, developmental delays, unintelligible speech, learning difficulties, sensory processing disorder, anxiety, depression, and sleep disorders are associated with technology overuse, and are increasing at an alarming rate."[6] We either accept this as if it were inevitable, or else we are too addicted to these same entertainments ourselves to care. We are disfiguring our children, and yet we seem impotent before the problem—trusting, I suppose, that someone else will take care of it for us by inventing a remedy.

We need to claim our independence from the mollycoddling technologies that hold us back from developing a sense of self-reliance and that keep us from the exercise of the resources within us. While being pampered now and again is a delight, living a pampered life is just downright boring, and even destructive to the human spirit. It tends to allow us to have unrealistic and overblown expectations, gives us a false impression of autonomy and freedom, and allows our minds to drift into veritable insanities. We need the adventure of being exposed. We need to find ourselves out on proverbial limbs, having to confront the real limitations of nature, and thus having to draw on our own resources, creatively solving difficulties with the means that are at hand as opposed to downloading the latest app or running to the local big box store to buy our way out of challenges. Such challenges have to be real and consequential. Video games and amusement parks, ropes courses and adventure getaways; these may help, but will not ultimately suffice. I honor those who do away with the many comforts and conveniences that technology has afforded us in order to discover these inner resources, to streamline their lives, to find largesse in what is lean, freedom in discipline, wellbeing in the uncomfortable, to know the world around them with less padding, and simply to face a worthy challenge. I can think of little that is more American than a love for this kind of moral

5. Xue, "Is There an App for That," http://harvardmagazine.com/2013/11/is-there-an-app-for-that.

6. Rowan, "Impact of Technology," para. 4. Rowan, a biologist and pediatric occupational therapist, is author of *Virtual Children: The Terrifying Truth About What Technology is Doing to Children.*

adventure in self-reliance, realized in informal, non-monetary reciprocity with one's neighbors and the land.

EXPERIENCE, LANGUAGE, AND THE ENVIRONMENT

To be sure, technology has not only furthered our disaffection from our own souls and bodies and from the challenges that bolster our development. It has also furthered our disaffection from the land, and so has extended the land's disfiguration. While we are more informed than ever about all the events throughout the world (a burden on our hearts if ever there was one) and are expected to have an opinion about all these events, we have yet lost touch with the ground beneath our feet. Where awareness of the environment once meant our survival, it has now become unnecessary in many cases. We are sheltered from the cold and from the heat by our machines. Where navigation once required a knowledge and awareness of the position of the stars and a keen sense of the land, our devices now tell us where to go, and we passively follow their directives.

One of the startling consequences of the Industrial Revolution has been a shift in the linguistic metaphors and categories through which we not only understand the world around us, but also our own selves and our relationship to that world. Our language has become technologized. More and more, we construct the metaphors and images by which we conceive of our lives from the processes of machines and computers as opposed to the organic processes of nature. Where once we may have thought of ourselves as being "lost in a fog," a palpable navigational experience contingent on weather and our environment, we now might say that our "hard drive has crashed" as if we were experiencing a technological malfunction. If anyone has listened to an old farmer speak, or considers the biblical idioms that once dominated the English language, one realizes how many of our linguistic metaphors, categories, and figures of speech by which we once made sense of ourselves and our world were founded in organic, natural images, images from life daily lived on the land. For example, the saying "one bad apple ruins the whole bunch" is a farming image. It contains within itself the knowledge necessary to store food without refrigeration in root cellars, and the need to check for bruised fruit that may go bad while in storage, causing all the others to go bad as well. The saying "a stitch in time saves nine" is meaningless in a consumeristic culture of disposal that replaces things rather than repairing them. "Separating the wheat from the chaff," "reap what you sow," "what's good for the goose is good for the gander," "the fox is guarding the hen house," "sowing your wild oats"—these are all phrases that arise from one's daily experience on the land, and they are largely meaningless when we do not know how to live on the land. For example, we often use the latter phrase to refer to certain irresponsible indulgences in a quasi-positive sense, but its original meaning was decidedly negative. Wild oats are a seed of no value, and so to sow them is not only a waste of time, but a waste of good land.

The languages of other cultures, many of which are disappearing under the thumb of global monoculture, also encode within themselves a similar awareness and appreciation of the environment, as well as a structure of values and ethical codes that shape and place bounds on that relationship. Scientists such as Stephen Hawking, Carl Sagan, and Richard Dawkins debunk the mythopoetic narratives that form the basis of indigenous and religious languages throughout the world. Meanwhile, these "backwards," "pre-scientific" cultures demonstrate a remarkable ability to observe and understand their environment. The Inuit, for an example, have built within their language seventy terms that account for differences in the quality of forming sea ice, twenty-five terms for the development of land-fast ice, and thirty-four terms for ice developing along the floe's edge.[7] The Haunoo in the Philippine archipelago can routinely identify over 1,500 varieties of plants and some 450 types of animals.[8] The Kapingamarangi Islanders utilize highly adapted fishing techniques that take into account the life cycles of over two hundred varieties of fish, and these techniques are enshrined in their linguistic and mytho-poetic traditions.[9] Who, then, is more scientifically in tune with his or her environment? Experience shapes language, and the direction that our language is taking indicates that we no longer experience ourselves as part of the land, as participants in larger organic processes with real imperatives, but as machines and computers. We have become disaffected from nature, lost in our specializations, a cloud of data, and our own heads. Not only this, but without a well-considered linguistic and mytho-poetic framework that shapes our uses of knowledge, we will too easily fall prey to the shallow and the ersatz, and to the lurking assumptions of secular liberalism that drives global consumerism, undermines

---

7. Bowers, *Mindful Conservatism*, 109.
8. Bowers, *Mindful Conservatism*, 110.
9. Bowers, *Mindful Conservatism*, 110.

local networks of reciprocity, and causes the disfiguration of nature. In order for these frameworks to be real and consequential, to bind together and to limit destructive behavior, they must be given to us through living traditions that are our own: face-to-face, heart-to-heart, person-to-person, generation-to-generation.

THE DATA THAT SCIENTISTS FAIL TO ACCOUNT FOR

Some of the brightest scientists our culture has produced have demonstrated right alongside their genius a remarkable idiocy. This idiocy, which functions as a kind of autism, is born of a near total disaffection from nature. Related to this is their propensity to further the Western liberal assumptions that disdain and disregard all things of the past—including "pre-scientific" civilizations themselves—as backwards, ignorant, repressive, and needless. Their work tends to further the subjection of organic, life-sustaining processes to the industrial process, the technological manipulation and commodification of nearly all aspects of life. Indeed, there is currently a near-seamless relationship between science, technology, and the corporate quest for global markets, and our educational systems, as well as our governments, seem to be happily aboard, shockingly even riding along in the back seat with the cart pulling the horse. These scientists routinely give voice to this disaffection, especially when reflecting on the technologies that are emerging from their research and the largely fantasized implications of these technologies in human society. By publicly reflecting in these ways, their role as scientific researcher and as futuristic fortuneteller is often confused, and the general public is left unable to discern between the two. Inevitably, the speculations to which such scientists give voice are almost always inspired by the Western, industrial, corporate schemata that they take for granted, and are duly peppered with all of the shallow optimism that accompanies such schemata. There is rarely hesitation or deep moral reflection on appropriate use, if any, of potential technologies, besides the promise of a "better future." As we tend to view scientists and their endeavor with a certain awe, and as scientists themselves are not in the least shy about claiming their own superiority over the ignorant masses,[10]

---

10. Carl Sagan, for an example, forwards the claim that all beliefs and values that cannot be investigated scientifically are mere superstition. Bowers, highlighting the incredible hubris in such a claim, points out that Sagan's category of superstition necessarily

the often-silly and ethically questionable details of their predictions and pontifications are too often obscured by our misplaced veneration.

By way of example, one of the ways in which scientists make futuristic pronouncements that are as silly as they are troubling is the idea that humans will be replaced by computers, as if we have no choice in the matter. This scenario, they would say, represents evolution; it is progress. Not only this, but computers will solve even that most sticky of all problems—mortality, which remains an unhappy insult in the face of human hubris and endeavor. If a person were to download into a computer all of the information in their brain, some would claim, they would then have realized eternal life. With such a technology, we will have defeated death, as if our bodies and all that they depend on had nothing to do with the life we delight in. American author, computer scientist, and inventor Ray Kurtzweil writes,

> There won't be mortality by the end of the twenty-first century. Not in the sense that we have known it. Not if you take advantage of the twenty-first century's brain-porting technology. Up until now, our mortality was tied to the longevity of our hardware. When the hardware crashed, that was it ... As we cross the divide to instantiate ourselves in our computational technology, our identity will be based on our evolving mind file ... Our mortality will be a matter of being sufficiently careful to make frequent backups.[11]

Not only do we see Kurtzweil utilizing purely technological metaphors to describe the organic human body and brain ("hardware"), but we witness here an understanding of human identity that amounts to nothing more than a walking conglomerate of data. In all of the instances we have been looking at throughout this work, we witness the reduction of the human nature. A human person is, in these worldviews, little more than a consuming, copulating, calculating being. This is a disfiguration of nature at its finest, and if we disfigure the human nature in this way, how much more will we disfigure the nature of all creatures, especially inanimate creatures?

Scientists such as Hans Moravec, Gregory Stock, and George Dyson follow similar lines as Ray Kurtzweil, making wild, futuristic predictions as if speaking from the infallible throne of science. Moravec, who served as

---

includes "the various forms of knowledge held by the majority of the world's population." It is knowledge that "has led to discoveries that Western science has only begun to recognize as important," such as indigenous knowledge of plants that forms the basis of many contemporary pharmaceuticals (Bowers, *Mindful Conservatism*, 78).

11. Kurtzweil, *Age of Spiritual Machines*, 128–29.

the principle research scientist at the Robotics Institute at Carnegie Mellon University and remains an adjunct faculty member there while working as chief scientist at Seegrid Corporation, believes that scientific research itself is dictated by evolution as if by an unseen hand, and that it is leading to a "postbiological world dominated by self-improving machines."[12] Not only can two men or two women have a child together, which is post-biological enough, but perhaps computers will also someday demand the right to marry in order to raise their young. This wonderful development will lead to a restructuring of society, Moravec predicts, where

> entire corporations will exist without any human employees or investors at all . . . our descendants will cease to work in the sense that we do now. They will probably occupy their days with a variety of social, recreational and artistic pursuits, not unlike today's comfortable retirees or the wealthy leisure classes.[13]

Given the highly specialized nature of his education, we should not be surprised that Moravec demonstrates a near total blindness to the Western, secular assumptions that shape his vision. He is unable or unwilling to consider the elitist provenance of his dreams, or that such a vision of the future may not be desirable to various cultural groups around the world. Nor is he willing to consider its effect on the environment and the natural resources that would presumably continue to support our endless leisure and artistic pursuits. While we wait for the manifestation of such a utopia as this, perhaps we might be able to keep our day jobs and live responsibly and sanely on the land that feeds us.

TECHNOLOGY AND FOOD

Because food represents our most basic connections with, and dependencies on, the land, and because agriculture represents the most fundamental use of land, the effects of the industrialization of food reveals the tendency of technology to further our disaffection from, and so disfiguration of, nature. Like the technocrats and scientists quoted above, agri-scientists and agri-businessmen are also prone to overly exuberant and ill-considered futuristic prophecies. In his provocative analysis of the state of American farming and culture, entitled *The Unsettling of America: Culture and Agriculture*,

---

12. Moravec, *Mind Children*, 8. See Bowers, *Mindful Conservatism*, 70.
13. Moravec, *Mind Children*, 135.

agrarian conservationist and prophet Wendell Berry quotes an article that appeared in a 1970 issue of National Geographic. The article's author, in what Berry sardonically calls "the glory of the true future-rapture," proclaims that "Fields will be larger, with fewer trees, hedges, and roadways. Machines will be bigger and more powerful . . . They'll be automated, even radio-controlled, with closed circuit TV to let an operator sitting on a front porch monitor what is going on . . . Weather control may tame hailstorm and tornado dangers . . . Atomic energy may supply power to level hills or provide irrigation water from the sea."[14] After a few pages of such quotes, Berry comments,

> The issue that is raised most directly by these farms-of-the-future . . . is that of total control . . . Nowhere is the essential totalitarianism and the essential weakness of the specialist mind more clearly displayed than in this ambition. Confronted with the living substance of farming—the complexly, even mysteriously interrelated lives on which it depends . . . —the agriculture specialist can think only of subjecting it to total control, of turning it into a machine.[15]

Generally, the story around food goes something like the following. Human population is increasing and available land is decreasing. Therefore, we have to produce more food on less land. Technology helps us to accomplish this. Agricultural technology, in the proficient hands of the agri-scientists and the agri-businessmen who fund them, will feed the world. They will take care of the problem for us, and we can go on living the lavish lives that we live while the rest of the world, under their influence, catches up. Rarely does such a narrative raise the question of conservation and right land use. Rarely, if ever, does this narrative include a denouncement of the waste of good, potentially productive land at the hands of irresponsible sprawl and bad community planning, nor does it consider the fact that most rural communities whose wealth once grew from its small farms have emptied out while the bulk of these farms have gone fallow. Countless rural Americans have been displaced not only by mechanized farming, but also by the popular disdain for their "backwards" way of life, and countless rural communities struggle under the burden of neglect. Perhaps I do not find it fulfilling in the least to sit on my porch idle all day, staring at a screen and

---

14. Billard, "Revolution in American Agriculture"; quoted in Berry, *Unsettling of America*, 70–71.

15. Berry, *Unsettling of America*, 74–75.

making a few adjustments on a joystick every now and again. Perhaps what fulfills me is a lively interaction with land and neighbor.

Anyone who lives in a community whose history is dominated by the family farm surely must have a different take on the current situation than the agri-businessmen who, like all businessmen, see the failure of the little guy as par for the course, the necessary sacrifice of progress. All around us, good farmland is turning to scrubland, while rural communities are leaking out the last of their young workforce—a long emptying-out that took hold during the Industrial Revolution—all of whom are going to the cities and the suburbs for jobs and the promise of leisure, glory, and all else that money can buy. The industrialization of agriculture has put the total amount of working farmland into the hands of a mere 1 percent of the population.[16] By comparison, in 1940 a little less than 25 percent of the total population were farmers. Census data indicates that this number continues to steadily decline while the average age of farmers is steadily rising.[17]

Relative to the overall US populace, the percentage of people residing in rural America has been falling sharply since the Industrial Revolution.[18] Rural people have been leaving rural areas.[19] In at least one report, tidings of rural growth have been published with hopeful tones, but the devil is in the details. According to a 2006 study by The University of New Hampshire's Carsey Institute, some rural areas are indeed growing, but likely with an influx of urbanites and retirees.[20] If so, few of these new arrivals will contribute meaningfully in the rural economy, and fewer still will live in close dependence on the land. The decline of farming opens the way for a new kind of rural diversity, but in the end, drives the knife deeper into the heart of rural life as farming and land-based rural economies give way to more urban models based on leisure activities, cash, and consumerism.[21] This so-called rural population growth may simply indicate the continued transformation of rural places into urban ones, or at best may amount to nothing over the long haul. Indeed, the most recent report that I can find

---

16. According to the latest available census data for farmers, from the 2012 census.

17. Dimitri et al., "20th Century Transformation," 3, fig. 1.

18. Johnson, *Demographic Trends*, 9, fig. 1. See also *Taking Stock*, 9, fig. 1.

19. Johnson, *Demographic Trends*, 1.

20. An upswing in immigrant populations in rural areas comes with some social and economic promise, especially if the second generation stays to raise families and participate meaningfully in the rural economy. See Johnson, *Demographic Trends*, 1.

21. Johnson, *Demographic Trends*, 1–2 (in the Executive Summary; see note above).

demonstrates an overall rural population decline, and not just as a percentage of the total US population, but as a demographic unto itself.[22] The title of a 2017 Bloomberg Opinion article seems to sum it up best: "Rural America is Aging and Shrinking: Technology and Diverging Values Widen the Gap Between Small-Town USA and Cities."[23] As far as farming is concerned, the more people who leave rural areas (or who populate rural areas as retirees and vacationers without putting traditional farmland to work), the fewer people are left to grow our nation's food. Farmers are burdened with the task of producing more food on larger acreages with less help. They become dependent on more technology to make the task possible. The more technology a farmer utilizes, the more dependent he or she becomes on outside inputs, and so the more financially strapped he or she becomes. A combine tractor alone, for an example, can cost a farmer as much as half a million dollars. In my town, that money would buy a family an exceedingly fine farm. Indebtedness and all of its woes have become commonplace on the American farm. Gone are the rural virtues of solvency and thrift. The farmer, like so many contemporary Americans, operates on credit, not only indebted to the banks and the financiers, but borrowing from his children by depleting the land.

The more financially strapped a farmer becomes, the less inclined he or she is to care for the long-term fertility of the land, especially when such care comes at the expense of short-term gains. Here begin many bad practices, which in time become normal practices. Encouraged by his financiers, the agri-businessmen, universities, and government officials, whose concern is profitability (always, they say, for the sake of the farmer), every inch of a farmer's land is put under production. Riparian buffers and habitat for other species who provide a biological balance to the land are sacrificed; the soil is given little rest and time for regeneration; beauty and diversity disappear from the farm. The farmer becomes a specialist, a factory worker. He buys his own food at the supermarket. The less inclined the farmer is to care for the long-term fertility of the land, the more dependent he or she becomes on outside inputs, such as fertilizers and pesticides, again upping the financial burden in a catch-22. These other inputs are needed to make up for the lost fertility of the land, the eroded and depleted topsoil, and the disease and pest problems inherent in the growing of vast monoculture

22. Cromartie, "Rural Areas," para. 1.
23. Fox, "Rural America," https://www.bloomberg.com/view/articles/2017-06-20/rural-america-is-aging-and-shrinking.

cash crops. Altogether, it is a recipe for ruin, and the system's great promise of food security is, like many such promises, built on the fantasy of unlimited technological and financial progress. In reality, it is a sham. While lining the pockets of agri-businessmen, its cheerleaders' rhetoric is characteristically devoid of any long-range, level-headed consideration. As long as we are fed for the moment, the promise will strike us as plausible. To believe the rhetoric is, at least, convenient, for we have better things to do with our time than to go out and grow some food. Technology will feed us, we tell ourselves. If there is a disaster, technology will save us.

But agribusiness is currently playing a losing game. For example, when considering the fossil fuel and other inputs farmers have become dependent on, it has been estimated that an industrial farmer puts in ten calories of energy for every one calorie of food he produces.[24] Technology, as far as agriculture is concerned, has made food production into a net loss endeavor; literally a futile, wasted effort. Our children and our children's children will know it. At the same time, and perhaps most importantly for those who would value human productiveness and liberty, year after year agriculture provides a viable living for fewer and fewer families. While the small family farms go fallow and their children move elsewhere, the giants join house to house and field to field in a spirit of monopoly.[25] We are spending the principal, and we have turned much of rural America, once prosperous and respectable, into a wasteland. We have made slums of small communities, or turned them into ghost towns, or are letting them become playgrounds for the city people who walk on the back of these wastes, have money and time to burn, and push local people out of their homelands by driving up land prices while leaving that land unproductive. They do the latter believing that it is the best thing to do, but it only betrays an inherent disaffection from the land. It demonstrates their idea of land as separate from themselves, something to be enjoyed from a comfortable distance, as if it were a terrarium. It betrays the fact that their livelihood has been derived elsewhere, and is not dependent on a direct interaction with the earth.

Finally, when we are not turning rural areas into ghost towns, terrariums, or resorts, we are turning rural areas into industrial zones. Polluted with farm chemicals, rural landscapes dominated by the large mechanized farm grow ugly in the sheer utility to which we have subjected them. They

---

24. Lott, "10 Calories In, 1 Calorie Out."
25. See Isa 5:8.

may have been, or might yet be, scarred by extractive industries such as timber and mining, and now we are scarring them with solar and wind "farms" so that we can feel good about ourselves while continuing to use too much energy in a wasteful life of consumption. As Wendell Berry has noted, "If we had an unlimited supply of solar or wind power, we would use that destructively, too."[26] This is so because we refuse to ask the question about the proper and improper use of things; about what good decisions and bad decisions are; about the virtues of limitation, responsibility, leanness, faithfulness, and sanity. It is so because we do not know what a good life is. Why should we, after all, be tied to the land or to anything in particular when we can grow fat in our cosmopolitanism and narcissistic adventures, overfed by an agricultural system that is supposedly the envy of the world? Never mind that it represents a net loss and totters precariously on the great, ravenous machine of industry, which is laying waste to our rural communities and their cultures, and spreading like a cancer abroad.

There has been much concern about the proverbial 1 percent of the population holding the majority of the wealth in our nation, but why are we not outraged that only 1 percent of our population is growing the majority of our food? Where is the true wealth of our nation but in her farmers? Why do we not reclaim our good land and put it to work responsibly? Why do we not strive to make the household into a place of production rather than consumption? Why do we not ask what we can do for ourselves rather than ask what the government or the corporations or the technologists will do for us? This is the surest way to generate resilient, independent, self-sustaining communities and thriving towns, and to increase liberty. Our rural lands, their health and productivity, are the root and source of urban health, not the other way around. Urban money will never save rural community, nor will urban values. To reclaim rural life and personal productivity would be the best way to leave that 1 percent of supposed wealth-holders in the dust. We cannot buy, we cannot invent, we cannot protest, and though much of this paper focuses on the power of the vote and why voting for one issue necessarily means voting for another, we ultimately cannot even vote our way out of our problems. Our politicians will reflect our culture. The roots of our problems lie in the integrity and in the character of the soil of our souls. The best thing the government could do is to resurrect some kind of Homestead Act with twenty-first-century qualifications, putting people back on the land while also ensuring

---

26. Berry, *Unsettling of America*, 15.

the activities engaged thereon are appropriate to particular landscapes and parcels, such as grazing in semiarid zones rather than plowing.[27] Regrettably, government is very unlikely to address in any abiding way the plight of rural America. Most governmental leaders take for granted the narrative of unlimited progress, for which the small farmer is just one of the necessary sacrifices, and tend to see land as a private financial investment and not as home, nor as country, not even as a fitting subject for our fidelity. Our fidelity, so we are told, should be to the providers of jobs and to the things, conveniences, and entertainments that they supply us with. I fear that, in an age so utterly conditioned by the consumerist mentality, officials would in any event be hard-pressed to find people willing to sacrifice their mobility, conveniences, cosmopolitanism, and grandiose visions of themselves and their destinies for a quotidian, settled life of responsible stewardship on the land. Indeed, the market that our officials support would not have it. Until we can value such a life, however—until the small landowner can again make a go at it on his holding—we will keep moving toward the demise of liberty into a deepening slavery to corporate hegemony.

Putting wilderness aside is a valuable land use for many reasons, but we must not mistake it to be the only goal for conservation and environmental action. We need to put people back on the land because the backbone of any nation that would promote liberty is the long-term fertility of the soil and the stability and independence of the people who work it. We need to put people back on the land, because when human intimacy with the land dies or is overwhelmed by the more common experience of disaffection from the land, the land and human culture itself will be disfigured, as is now the case. In 1785, Thomas Jefferson wrote to fellow Founding Father and statesman John Jay, "Cultivators of the earth are the most valuable citizens. They are the most vigorous, the most independent, the most virtuous, and they are tied to their country and wedded to its liberty and interests by the most lasting bonds. As long, therefore, as they can find employment in this line, I would not convert them into mariners, artisans, or anything else."[28] In another letter addressed to Founding Father, jurist, and legal scholar John Blair Jr. in 1787, Jefferson reiterated his sentiment,

---

27. One of the causes of the Dust Bowl was that semiarid lands, which should have remained in grass, were instead subjected to intensive plowing. When drought struck, there was nothing to hold the soil.

28. Jefferson, "John Jay," para. 1.

"The pursuits of agriculture [are] the surest road to affluence and best preservative of morals."[29]

Global businessmen have attacked the very spine of America by attacking the independence of the farmer, making the farmer dependent on a host of outside, manufactured inputs, turning him into a specialist factory worker, and putting him into undue competition with foreigners. In my hometown, a mountain farming community whose topography necessitates good stewardship of the land, small holdings, and diversified agricultural activity, I lament to see anyone, but a farmer especially, at the local supermarket buying lamb from Australia or vegetables from Mexico, particularly because his neighbor (or he himself) is likely struggling to find a market for his own produce. Jefferson also wrote, "If we can but prevent the government from wasting the labours of the people, under the pretence of taking care of them, they must become happy."[30] We can expand his words to include not only government but also the patronizing corporate technologists, with all of their promises and pretenses of giving us a better life, who would grow fat on our labor and waste our land until cheaper labor and more land to waste is found elsewhere. We can do better. But we must be willing to work, renounce our fascination with glamour and self-indulgence, and be responsible citizens, tied to land and country.

---

29. Jefferson, "John Blair," para. 1.
30. Jefferson, "Thomas Cooper," para. 1.

Chapter 7

Coming Home

Only a man harrowing clods
In a slow silent walk
With an old horse that stumbles and nods
Half asleep as they stalk.

Only thin smoke without flame
From the heaps of couch-grass;
Yet this will go onward the same
Though Dynasties pass.[1]
—Thomas Hardy

Throughout this work, I have highlighted a pattern. It is a pattern that is part and parcel of the process of industrialization, urbanization, and consumerism, marked by the tendency to demean and devalue what is traditional, settled, lean, and limited. Mistaking novelty for freedom, self-indulgence for liberty, and all change for progress, we are rapidly undermining the relationships, obligations, and virtues that make for stable, healthy societies. Not only this, but we are at the same time producing a

---

1. Hardy, "Breaking of Nations," 511.

broad disaffection from the land. This happens in part through the transfer of the fealties of the majority of the population from a direct obligation to the land itself to a dependency on consumer goods, jobs and the providers of jobs, and a faceless, homogenous, globalized market economy in general. When direct dependencies on the land and one's neighbors are undermined, the order of human values are turned upside-down. The land becomes an abstraction, and if it is valued at all, it is valued abstractly, the way we might value an interesting idea. As an idea—the "environment," "nature," "the outdoors"—the land becomes less real. Our daily lives have been abstracted from the fact of the land through the patronizing benevolence of industry and its promise of leisure and endless abundance. Technology and our uses of it shield and isolate us from direct, reciprocal relationships with nature. We therefore no longer experience the land as a living reality, within which we ourselves are, and always will be (despite our machines and conveniences), a dependent participant. Thus, in a certain trend of environmental rhetoric, taking care of the land becomes little more than removing ourselves from it. Wendell Berry puts it nicely: "The conservationist congratulates himself, on the one hand, for his awareness of the severity of human influence on the natural world. On the other hand, in his own contact with that world, he can think of nothing else but to efface himself."[2] This is because he is himself ultimately disaffected from the land, and all disaffection from the land will lead to its disfiguration.

We have also noted how this disaffection from the land goes hand in hand with a disfiguration of our bodies and our humanity; how the abuse, misuse, and heedless exploitation of our bodies and the bodies of others is intricately interwoven with the same exploitation of the earth. We simply cannot advance a laissez-faire morality when it comes to our personal lives and then call for restraints and good order when it comes to public concerns and the influence of the market on the land. What we get when we make this separation is the strange but commonplace specter of the person who believes it is right to care for the environment while living in a vast house in a vast suburb. Perhaps this person owns another house in the country, effectively removing that house from local use, emptying out rural towns, and driving rural people further into poverty by unduly elevating real estate values. Our subject might commute an hour or more to work, and work for any number of corporations or organizations whose activities directly efface the earth and advance the disfiguring effects of global

2. Berry, *Unsettling of America*, 33.

industrialization. He or she may be well invested in these kinds of activities, securing a comfortable retirement directly from them, while a few degrees of separation and popular practice makes it all seem good and natural. We might get the environmentalist who talks eloquently about the need for landowners to appreciate that the influence of their actions on their private holdings do not stop at the boundary line. In the next breath, they will support abortion, pornography, or other sexual indulgences—either implicitly or explicitly—by arguing that what people do in their private lives with their own private bodies is of no public consequence; that it is no one else's business how they live. They might speak of our need to commit wholeheartedly and make sacrifices in order to save a certain species of animal or plant while they themselves are either emotionally unable or unwilling to commit to a spouse, religion, cultural context with an intact history, community service organization, or stable home. Public and private is a false division; how we live our own lives in the marketplace as well as in the home, when we are on duty and off duty, matters deeply. We are society, always. If we are going to value, care for, and tend to the land, then we must value, care for, and tend to our own souls and bodies. We must tend to the quality of our relationships with other souls and bodies. We must esteem and guard the integrity of both self and other. Our relationships must be shaped by nurturance and obligation, by a heroic commitment to community and place, not by consumerism, vagrancy, and a commitment only to one's own ideas, pleasures, and fancies.

We might say that the real question of conservation is the question of use. To be sure, we have no other choice but to use the good things of this world. We use our bodies and our minds every day. If we are to eat, to be clothed, to have a roof over our heads and warmth in the winter, if we are to make a living doing anything at all, then we must use the land. If we are to ensure that our children's children will have these things and will themselves have meaningful livelihoods, then we must use the land well. Using anything well is first to know it intimately, and this means knowing it within its context. Any parcel of land is a part of a larger landscape. We must be intimate with both. Given this intimacy, what kinds of uses are appropriate to it? What kinds of uses would not be appropriate? To use anything well is to honor what it already is and does and to build on those virtues, and to leave it as good or better than one has found it. Therefore, to use anything well is to nurture it as well. Making a living is not merely about making money, as if all profitable endeavors were in the end equal, or all endeavors good if they are fiscally profitable. Indeed, the more an endeavor is fiscally profitable, and the more an endeavor feeds our vices, the less inclined we will be to ask the question of proper use, and the more inappropriate and grotesque our endeavors will become.

We find, then, that the question of use does not ultimately satisfy the question of conservation. Use itself, if it is to be responsible, must be guided by a larger concern, a larger experience, a larger consideration than usefulness and convenience alone. We cannot merely ask how we will use the land and other lives for our own comforts and survival because, in the real world, we ourselves will also be used, not only by others, but also by the land. No one can escape being used in this way. Use is reciprocal, and the more we allow room for this reciprocity—the more we allow ourselves to be used and to be of use—then the more we realize that the ultimate question is not only about appropriate, generous use, but about reciprocity, about relationship. All rights are relational; there can be no rights for anyone if our exercise of them remains indifferent to the obligations of relationship. What will the quality of our relationships be? Will convenience and luxury be the only pilots and mediators of our relationships, or will our relationships be guided by genuine love? Our colloquial uses of this term "love" tend to cheapen it. What I mean by love is a genuine relationship with reality, a relationship that is necessarily transformative and humbling—sometimes painfully so—precisely because it is a genuine engagement with reality, as opposed to an engagement solely with the built and invented environment, our own whims and fancies included. Because we are talking about a relationship that is a genuine engagement with reality, we are talking about a relationship in which we do not get to call the shots. There are many givens in such a relationship. While we do not create it or make it up, we can nurture it, participate in it, and surrender to it, for it is a communion. In other words, love is a relationship that can only be found and forged in humility and limitation, which comprise the only way to authentic communion. When we are full of ourselves, when we think of ourselves as the sole creators and sustainers of our lives, then we crush all possibility for such communion.

We witness in our time the increasing inability for people to conceive of relationships of love. It is a deeply tragic symptom of our disaffection from land and community. This tendency is perhaps most noticeable in popular scholarship, where history (for an example) and the often tight and consequential associations of cultures are routinely interpreted almost solely through the concepts of dominance and subjection. As we have discussed throughout this work, such narratives are forwarded in an effort to deflate and devalue all that is of the past, all that is traditional. Its aim is to advance some perceived heroic (even if tragic, rootless, and cynical) march into an imagined utopian future and its promise of liberation from all of the insults of human embeddedness in time, place, family, gender, and community. Habitually, without discernment, and full of a maniacal hubris, these narratives write off as repressive and backwards not only past cultural norms, but also the norms of nature herself. It is in the interest of the marketers, the technologists, and the monopolists that we have no history, roots, cultural traditions, or obligations except to the market economy and to the jobs and products they offer. Meanwhile, such a program leaves us in a spiritual vacuum, seemingly devoid of the vision of love. We cannot envision order, authority, and obligation without domination, or self-giving without submission and addiction. We are blind to the fact that obedience and freedom can exist in harmony; that limitation is the only way to wholeness. We do not know the reconciling power of love.

I do not suggest the preservation of all things historical and traditional, as if our ancestors were somehow immune to moral corruption. They were not immune, as we are not immune. I do argue, however, that tradition is part and parcel to human life and existence, and that our best bet for integrity is to walk on the shoulders of those who have gone before us, while remembering that our children will do the same. Otherwise, we will find that we have no ground under our feet, and that we leave even less ground for our children. We will find that we are rootless and dangerous in our instability. Summing up a study on conservation and New England fisheries, Judd notes with some regret that, "Ultimately, the small scale . . . fisheries succumbed to the forces of large-scale capitalism,"[3] requiring large-scale regulations, which in turn perpetuate large-scale use. Still, it was the local sense of the commons, handed down through generations of reciprocity with the land, that drove and informed the conservation movement. He reflects that "Republican values, resting on patriotic traditions and democratic economic structures, buttressed an abiding sense of antimonopoly— and to a degree antimodern—feeling . . . Economic change is everywhere destabilizing, but traditional norms can show a remarkable persistence and vitality even in the face of a fully developed commercial economy."[4] One

---

3. Judd, *Common Lands*, 261.
4. Judd, *Common Lands*, 262.

of Judd's points here is that the traditional value structures, formed and handed down through a common life sustained by generational partnership with the land, go a long way toward protecting local land users from undue dependencies on destructive or at least indifferent market forces, and from undue ignominy under the conglomerates that such forces tend to produce and perpetuate. It is this kind of reliance on the land, coupled with a love for liberty and relationships formed under the banner of mutual obligation, that moves a local community to protect its land resources in the face of outside exploitation, and to develop localized moral structures to ensure the integrity of the commons. Sound forests grow on the deep loams of their own history, and sound human communities do the same. Besides, if we do not own the good of our ancestors, how can we atone for their sins? Let us not be afraid to be limited, for in limitation we will find belonging, not only to a place, but also to a people and to the earth herself. In belonging, in reconciliation and reintegration, our disaffection might be turned to affection, and nature's disfiguration to its transfiguration.

Our longing for unlimited life, our intuition that there is something beyond the bounds and constraints of created existence, is not a complete fiction. There is, indeed, a life beyond. There is a life that is unlimited in which we can partake and of which we can drink deeply. This life, though, does not belong to us. It does not belong to the created order, and we certainly cannot create it ourselves. The more we try to create it, take hold of it, and control it, the further from it we are, and the narrower of heart we become. Though this unlimited life is the source of creation, it is wholly other than creation. Though it is the ground of creation, it is wholly above it. This life belongs to God, who alone is eternal and boundless. To participate in this unlimited life is not to destroy limited nature, but to unite the limited with the unlimited without mixing or abolishing them. In other words, we participate in this life through the union of time and eternity, of the limits of created, natural life with the unconditioned life of God. This is where the sequel to this essay, *The Transfiguration of Nature*, will begin. Our entrance into this life, however, is in renouncing the sundry programs that seek to co-opt God and impudently, imprudently, tragically seek to make ourselves into little, atomized gods in his stead, projecting our own limited egos into an infinity of our imagination. Such an infinity as this—the unlimited of the limited—cannot ever be complete. It cannot ever be whole or provide contentment, because it always can be added to, at least in our imaginations. I can always get one more thing, have one more success, make one more dollar, subdue one more lover, reject one more condition. This is not the way to life without end. Union with unlimited life begins in returning, with great humility and love, to the limited, contingent dependency that is the truth of our lives as members of created existence. We have to come home.

COMING HOME

We have spent much time focused on the forces that work to undermine human connection, relationships of reciprocity, and genuine affinity to the land. As such, this book has taken a path that has largely been a negative one. I have offered a critique of certain assumptions, narratives, practices, and movements that I feel are antithetical to a life of sanity and stability, and so to the environmental imperative. The critique is necessary, because these assumptions and practices are forwarded alongside the environmental cause as if representing an equal matter. At least in the voting booth, we cannot bolster one without bolstering the other. Any critique that would have meaning must emerge from positives, from standards and experiences that have presented themselves as better ways. The standard behind my critique is what I would call a good life. It is a life, however difficult, whose rough edges are nevertheless softened by affinity, friendship, mutuality, belonging, productivity, and broad intelligence that does not specialize in any particular subject, but rather observes the total movement of life, seeking sources and ends. It is a life moved by obligations larger than itself. Such a life is not an idea or ideology. It is realized only in authentic relationship with what is real, and not in ideas and ideals. We all must eat, be clothed, be sheltered, and belong. If we begin to ask what the sources of the things that meet these needs are, we will be led by a process of elimination away from the various and sundry middlemen of globalized, mechanized society and find ourselves in a face-to-face, body-to-body encounter with the land. We will likely also find ourselves in a rural place, from whence is extracted the majority of the raw materials of our built environment. We will find this rural place largely forgotten, drained perhaps not only of its resources, but also of its people. The good life begins by returning to sources, however dilapidated they have become in our neglect of them. The good life begins in understanding this neglect, and in tasting the pain of it. The elitist dream of leisure and luxury, of being waited on by the labors of foreign peasants and by machines of every kind, the elitist dream of influence and power and endless pleasures, must crumble in this pain. The snobbish, urbane neglect of our embeddedness in nature, of rural places, the neglect of human labor and human affinity with the dirt, must end. Though we must protect them from the wanton, grasping hands of industry—including, I would say, the wind and solar power industries—these forgotten places must not merely be set aside from human contact, conserved as if in a museum. These places must rather become again a home to people who will thrive on and in them, and so a home to people who will love them, care for them, and safeguard them. They must become places of life, where people, gathered around the common task of steadfast subsistence, sweat together in the fertile field that feeds them.

In the first pages of *The Unsettling of America*, Wendell Berry speaks about the restless, expansive, exploitative propensities that drove the colonization of the New World. Yet, he also identifies another tendency, albeit for him a minority one, which is the tendency to settle and to belong, a leaning toward what Berry calls "domestic permanence."[5] He reads this domestic impulse in the letters and the preoccupations of America's Founding Fathers, men like Thomas Jefferson and George Washington, who were constantly writing home concerned about the plantings and the affairs of the farmstead, and who spoke eloquently about the central place of the smallholder in a society that would be sound and truly free.[6] Though the expansive push of colonization would bring a demise to the settled Native Americans (something for which we are yet to atone through public policy), to underestimate the influence that a desire for a peaceable, stable life had on European settlement in North America would be a grave historical error. From the top, colonization was indeed driven by monarchs, commercial groups, and other elites. On the ground, however, colonization was effected by settlers, the unfortunate poor looking for financial independence through the husbandry of their own small parcels, emigrants seeking religious liberty and the same economic self-sufficiencies by the same means, and slaves who would, in their own turn, seek similar ends, having finally gained their freedom. The initial dream on the ground was for a settled life lived in peace, husbanding one's own holding, and belonging to one's neighbors. Judd's painstaking historical analysis demonstrates that, at least in the case of northern New England, it was the local land owners

---

5. Berry, *Unsettling of America*, 15.

6. See, for an example, the quote from Jefferson in the heading for chapter 2 of this book.

and users, fortified by their traditions of reciprocity, local self-sufficiency, and love for liberty, who served as the bulwark and ground of the conservation movement in that place.[7] Ties to the land created a repugnance toward commercial hegemony, outside speculation, and elitist monopolization. It was the natural conservatism of the people, not their liberality, which furthered and shielded these ties.

According to Berry, one of the leading safeguards of liberty in America was the imperative "that as many as possible should share in the ownership of the land and thus be bound to it by economic interest, by the investment of love and work, by family loyalty, by memory and tradition."[8] The freed slaves of the 1860s hoped for forty acres on which to settle, to work, and to call home. The Homestead Act of 1862 also gave official expression to this goal by allotting 160-acre parcels for settlement. It was the dream of countless immigrants to share in this ownership and productivity, while we are now content to expect government and corporations to take care of land stewardship for us, happy to rent in the cities and go to our country "homes" to play. This is not in any way an argument against government ownership of certain land resources, such as national parks, nor is it an argument against strong governmental leadership in environmental regulation. It is only to say that we all must play an active part if we are to conserve and love our land; we must go back to it to know it and to love it. Democracy in America has always been wedded to the land, our common bond. Land fails to be a common bond, however, when the majority of the population is disaffected from it. This disaffection makes the people prone to the whims of commercial cartels; it is destructive of American liberty.

Land and houses are not financial investments, nor are they resorts or playgrounds. They are homes. Home is the only place where the good life can take root and grow. Home is the only place where we will again find connections that move beyond the range of our reach. That is to say, home is where connections will find us, where we will be touched, sought-out, and changed by what is beyond our power to pick and to choose. A marriage is not a marriage if it is reliable only in the good times. A marriage becomes a marriage precisely when the hard times hit, when the continued communion with another demands something of us, perhaps all of us; not only when we are expanded by the relationship, but chiefly when we are limited by it. When a sacrifice is demanded of us, and when we willingly

---

7. Judd, *Common Lands*.
8. Berry, *Unsettling of America*, 16.

offer it, however flinchingly, this is where the mystery of love deepens. This is true for community, for religious and other cultural commitments, and for home.

Home for us, therefore, will be a tremendous challenge. To find it and to remain in it will be a pilgrimage. Home calls into question some of the most dear assumptions and presumptions of our day—mobility, social and economic advancement, the headiness of recognition and influence, the rush of power, the coolness of being up-to-the-minute, the flash of the rat race, the superciliousness of convenience and ease. As we disengage from all of these structures, though they be false and crumbling, we will totter and grope. The pain of this disorientation will be furthered by the reluctance of those who have never left home to receive those who are trying to find it; their reluctance is understandable, given the tendency of many newcomers to storm into stable communities with a sundry list of agendas that are alien and out of place. In my town, for example, a group of transplants (of which I am one in my community) are diligently working to get all of those who own a second home in the area to register to vote here rather than in the places where they live and work. This effort can only be called a type of colonialism, where our local representatives will not be representing the local majority at all, but absentee landowners. This undertaking goes against the primal assumption of democracy, that the people of any given place be represented in government by a duly elected official. That we can vote where we own property but do not live and work is a clear demonstration of our disaffection from home and place, as well as of the general disjunction and dislocation of our lives. Such behavior is an assault on the kind of being-at-home that I am talking about here.

It is not voting that fosters communal resilience. Resilience in the local community comes from common life, dependencies, and obligations, shared traditions and landscapes. It requires that people be willing to involve themselves in one another's lives. It requires that relationships be more than relationships of convenience, preference, and identity. Instead, it requires relationships of need and reciprocity. When we know we need one another and the land, then we are bound to care and to respond to one another and to the land. People need to involve themselves in the local community, and not just by fighting political battles. When transplants to rural areas are willing to make their new locale a true home and have shown that here is where they put their money down; to contribute meaningfully in the local economy, not only by who they hire to do their work for them, but also by their own work and productivity, then they deserve to be called locals. Rural communities should in fact have public celebrations where they officially adopt such persons as one of their own, in much the same way that some Native American tribes have adopted outsiders as one of their own. Unfortunately, stubbornness from the side of rural inhabitants often makes this integration difficult, even when it is well-earned and when it would strengthen local resilience.

The land, however, will receive the one who loves it. The one who loves the land will find a home if she stays, forsaking all others. To keep faith to a place is to keep faith to all places, for by being faithful to the one we are being faithful to all. There can be no so-called global places, only particular places; no global villages, only actual villages. This is not to deny a connection between particular places and other particular places. It is merely to say that we care for all of them only by caring for one of them. I love womankind by my exclusive fidelity to my wife. If I were not to love womankind in this way, I would be reducing womankind to something unworthy of such fidelity and faithfulness. Generalizations lead to vagaries, vagaries lead to confusion and diminishments, and confusion and diminishments lead to disaffection and disfiguration. Only in particularities are we empowered to live responsibly. To live responsibly in particularities is fidelity and faithfulness. It is only by consenting to the limitation of particularities that we can properly participate in the whole.

A CONCLUDING ANECDOTE

A recent conversation, however brief it was, serves as a good concluding anecdote to this work. It happened at a conference, a gathering for clergy. I was fixing myself a cup of tea and could not help overhearing a lively exchange at the table next to the tea bar where I was standing. The people in the small group were discussing the recent events in Charlottesville, Virginia,[9] particularly the reactionary censorship of the so-called Confederate flag in its wake. Just to throw in a balancing perspective, I offered, "Well, you know, the Confederate flag *is* a symbol of treason. I don't know why any self-respecting American would want to fly it." One of the men

---

9. Referencing an August 12, 2017 Neo-Nazi public event that turned into a violent confrontation with counter demonstrators. Besides bearing American and Nazi flags, they also bore so-called Confederate flags—a near-laughable (if it were not so tragic) confusion of symbols if ever there were one.

got very angry. Standing up, he said, "Well, this is America, and if someone wants to fly a Confederate flag or a Nazi flag, then God bless them!" I only said, "God cannot bless Nazism," and turned away from the conversation. I am ashamed to say that this man was himself a priest. It is no wonder that Christianity has born some condemnation as being at least an accomplice to a very huge social and political problem in contemporary America, though a part of me empathizes with this man's frustration at the ahistorical, contemptuous, and culturally iconoclastic liberal agendas that have surely put him on the defensive. In very real ways that too many Americans are unwilling to consider, these agendas threaten his religious and cultural freedoms. Still, he was only reacting when what he needed to do most was some quiet reflecting.

This same man would not be able to bless an abortionist, nor even bless a same-sex wedding. But here he was, suggesting that God can bless Nazism, or that God can bless our nation if her people are stained by this hateful ideology. The duplicity of this man's reaction is typical of all political camps. He was blindly following the confused political agendas of his party, for him the so-called conservatives (while actually taking a libertarian stance on this issue); he was not thinking about the broader implications of his stance at all. He was too intellectually and morally lazy to consider the fact that traditional American values and Nazism, let alone Nazism and the gospel, cannot exist side by side. They are mutually exclusive in the same way that abortion, the wanton use of our bodies, and the proliferation of and profiteering from assault weapons, for a few examples, are incongruent not only with the gospel, but also with creation care and the conservationist cause. Equally exclusive of one another is a pro-life stance with both an anti-environment stance and a reactionary stance against a clear, due process that would make for responsible gun ownership. What is pro-life about degrading the environment? If more pro-lifers were willing to ask this question, more liberals would be willing to take them seriously. What is pro-life about weapons? What is better to toss away, a gun collection or unborn children? If American citizens have the right to arms, then they must first prove themselves responsible citizens.[10] We can say the same

---

10. The understanding of the right to bear arms has undergone the same degenerative process as understandings of property rights and rights of free speech, on which we have focused more fully in this work. The Second Amendment was not popularly understood as license for individuals to bear arms privately, but was connected to public service and the welfare of the people. As it states, "A well regulated Militia, being necessary to the security of a free State, the right of the people to keep and bear Arms, shall not

about a pro-life, pro-family, pro-community, pro-jobs, pro-culture/religion stance and the support of an unregulated, unchecked globalized market that clearly undermines and devalues these very things. They are mutually exclusive.

We have to conclude, then, that our political and moral categories are direly confused, and it is in the interest of those who profit most from this confusion that they stay confused. As for the priest, he forgets that, as a priest, his citizenship is primarily in God's kingdom, and only secondarily in the American empire, though he is charged to live in peace in the latter.[11] He has lost his grounding in the gospel for the sake of a worldly agenda, that of the so-called and wrongly called American "conservatives." As for the citizen who does not have a commitment to the gospel, his or her ability to reflect fully on the consequences of the various moral and social stances he or she takes seems equally confused and blunted. Focusing on issues as isolated matters, focusing on individuals and their sundry identities, focusing on the expediencies and whims of the moment, we have become blind to bigger pictures; we have become issue specialists and have lost a comprehensive moral and social vision for ourselves as a people. We do not recognize nor do we honor the relationships and the contexts that necessitate obligation, clarity of reflection, comprehensiveness of action, and self-restraint. We have fallen into a dangerous and dualistic political scheme whose two parties see as their sole agenda the contradiction of the other. This scheme is bolstered, and I would say in part caused, by the media, so incapable of nuance and slow consideration. At the same time, both

---

be infringed." The State of Texas, for example, once prohibited the carrying of dangerous weapons. When this law was challenged in the 1894 case *Miller v. Texas* on the grounds that this law denied Mr. Miller of his constitutional right under the Second Amendment, the State of Texas upheld its law, able to cite a host of legal precedents for doing so. "In his motion for a rehearing, however, defendant claimed that the law of the State of Texas forbidding the carrying of weapons and authorizing the arrest without warrant . . . was in conflict with the Second and Fourth amendments to the Constitution of the United States, one of which provides that the right of the people to keep and bear arms shall not be infringed, and the other of which protects the people against unreasonable searches and seizures. We have examined the record in vain, however, to find where the defendant was denied the benefit of any of these provisions, and, even if he were, it is well settled that the restrictions of these amendments operate only upon the federal power, and have no reference whatever to proceedings in state courts. *Barron v. Baltimore*, 7 Pet. 243; *Fox v. Ohio*, 5 How. 410; *Twitchell v. Commonwealth*, 7 Wall. 321; *Justices v. Murray*, 9 Wall. 274; *United States v. Cruikshank*, 92 U. S. 542, 92 U. S. 552; *Spies v. Illinois*, 123 U. S. 131." See Miller v. Texas, 153 U.S. 535 (1894).

11. See Phil 3:7, Rom 12:18, and 1 Pet 2:17 for examples.

parties form their arguments within the same mistaken or at least deficient liberal and libertarian, individualistically biased notional framework about rights. The only difference between the two parties is that they apply these notions as it suits their whims, and often merely to contradict, outdo, and defeat the other, as if we could somehow avoid contradicting and defeating ourselves by doing so. It is time to stop this madness. It is time to get clear, not only for the sake of the environment, this great creation, and all of the marvelous creatures whom we share it with, but also for the sake of our continued society.

It is time to come home again; to come home to this land, home to our neighbor's company, home to ourselves, our sanity, our integrity, our bodies, our places. It is time to come home again; to emerge out of the underworlds of our disaffection from human relationships and the land that has so marked the latter modern mind, for this disaffection leads to our disfiguration and to the disfiguration of nature. It is time to come home again; to return from the outer spaces of global dreaming, laissez-faire liberalism, and elitist fantasies of endless wealth and leisure, to return to the quotidian work of nurture, to the moral challenge of self-mastery, and to the joy of true productivity and belonging that is ours for the taking right where we are. In short, it is time to be conservative, and so to conserve.

Bibliography

"2012 Census Highlights." https://www.agcensus.usda.gov/Publications/2012/Online_Resources/Highlights/Farm_Demographics/.

"Abortion Is a Common Experience for U.S. Women, Despite Dramatic Declines in Rates." https://www.guttmacher.org/news-release/2017/abortion-common-experience-us-women-despite-dramatic-declines-rates.

"Against Equality: Queer Critiques of Gay Marriage." http://www.againstequality.org/stuff/against-equality-queer-critiques-of-gay-marriage/.

Alexis, Jonas E. "Ayn Rand's Objectivism and Sexual Calculus (Part 1)." *Veterans Today*, May 24, 2013. http://www.veteranstoday.com/2013/05/24/ayn-rands-objectivism-and-sexual-calculus-part-i/.

Annual Report of the Secretary of the Massachusetts Board of Agriculture. Boston: Massachusetts Board of Agriculture, 1887.

Anthony, Susan B. "Social Purity." http://www.pbs.org/stantonanthony/resources/index.html?body=social_purity.html.

Augustine of Hippo. *The City of God (de civitate dei)*. Translated by William Babcock. Hyde Park, NY: New City, 2012.

Berry, Wendell. *The Unsettling of America: Culture & Agriculture*. Berkeley: Counterpoint, 2015.

Billard, Jules B. "The Revolution in American Agriculture." *National Geographic*, February 1970.

Bowers, C. A. *Mindful Conservatism: Rethinking the Ideological and Educational Basis of an Ecologically Sustainable Future*. Lanham: Rowman & Littlefield, 2003.

Brighouse, Harry, and Adam Swift. *Family Values: The Ethics of Parent-Child Relationships*. Princeton: Princeton University Press, 2014.

Bryce, Emma. "America's Greenest Presidents." *Green: Energy, the Environment and the Bottom Line* (blog), *New York Times*, September 20, 2012. http://green.blogs.nytimes.com/2012/09/20/americas-greenest-presidents/?_r=0.

Buckley, William F., Jr. *Happy Days Were Here Again: Reflections of a Libertarian Journalist*. New York: Random House, 1993.

Burke, Edmund. *The Writings and Speeches of Edmund Burke, Volume III: Party, Parliament and the American War–1794*. Edited by Warren M. Elofson et al. Oxford: Clarendon, 1996.

Cleary, John. "The Interview: Dr. Hunter Madsen and the Homosexual Agenda." http://www.abc.net.au/radio/programs/sundaynights/the-interview-dr-hunter-madsen-and-the-homosexual-agenda/7738634.

Bibliography

Cory, Donald Webster. *The Homosexual in America*. New York: Greenberg, 1951.

"Court Rules Bakery Illegally Discriminated Against Gay Couple." http://aclu-co.org/court-rules-bakery-illegally-discriminated-against-gay-couple/.

Cromartie, John. "Rural Areas Show Overall Population Decline and Shifting Regional Patterns of Population Change." *Amber Waves*, September 5, 2017. https://www.ers.usda.gov/amber-waves/2017/september/rural-areas-show-overall-population-decline-and-shifting-regional-patterns-of-population-change/.

DeFries, Ruth, et al. "Deforestation Driven by Urban Population Growth and Agricultural Trade in the Twenty-first Century." *Nature Geoscience* 3 (2010) 178–81. http://www.nature.com/ngeo/journal/v3/n3/full/ngeo756.html.

Dimitri, Carolyn, et al. "The 20th Century Transformation of U.S. Agriculture and Farm Policy." https://ageconsearch.umn.edu/bitstream/59390/2/eib3.pdf.

Evelyn, John. *Sylva, Or A Discourse of Forest-Trees and the Propagation of Timber*. 4th ed. London: Doubleday, 1908. http://www.gutenberg.org/files/20778/20778-h/20778-h.htm.

Fox, Justin. "Rural America is Aging and Shrinking: Technology and Diverging Values Widen the Gap Between Small-Town USA and Cities." *Bloomberg*, June 20, 2017. https://www.bloomberg.com/view/articles/2017-06-20/rural-america-is-aging-and-shrinking.

Freyfogle, Eric T. *Agrarianism and the Good Society: Land, Culture, Conflict, and Hope*. Lexington: University Press of Kentucky, 2007.

———. *The Land We Share: Private Property and the Common Good*. Washington, DC: Island, 2003.

———. *Why Conservation is Failing and How It Can Regain Ground*. New Haven: Yale University Press, 2006.

Friedman, Edwin H. *Failure of Nerve: Leadership in the Age of the Quick Fix*. New York: Church Publishing, 2007.

Gibson, Campbell. *American Demographic History Chartbook: 1790-2000*. N.p.: self-pub, 2010. http://demographicchartbook.com/wp-content/uploads/2015/11/Gibson-DemographicChartbook.pdf.

Gorman, Michael J. "Abortion and the Early Church." https://incommunion.org/2004/11/28/abortion-and-the-early-church/.

Gottlieb, Robert. *Forcing the Spring: The Transformation of the American Environmental Movement*. Washington, DC: Island, 2005.

Hamilton, Andy. "Conservatism." https://plato.stanford.edu/entries/conservatism/.

Hardy, Thomas. "In Time of 'Breaking of Nations.'" *Collected Poems of Thomas Hardy*. London: Macmillan, 1932.

Harris, John. "Spare a Thought for the Late Unlamented One-Nation Tory." *The Guardian*, April 14, 2013. https://www.theguardian.com/commentisfree/2013/apr/14/thatcher-legacy-one-nation-conservatism.

Hays, Samuel P. *Conservation and the Gospel of Efficiency: The Progressive Conservation Movement, 1890–1920*. Reprint, Pittsburgh: University of Pittsburgh Press, 1999.

Heacox, Kim. *Visions of a Wild America*. Washington, DC: National Geographic Society, 1996.

"History of Zoophilia." https://en.wikipedia.org/wiki/History_of_zoophilia.

Housing Assistance Council. *Taking Stock: Rural People, Poverty, and Housing in the 21st Century*. Washington, DC: Housing Assistance Council, 2012. http://www.ruralhome.org/storage/documents/ts2010/ts_full_report.pdf.

Bibliography

"Human Population: Lesson Plans." http://www.prb.org/Publications/Lesson-Plans/HumanPopulation/Urbanization.aspx.

"Industrialization—Family." http://family.jrank.org/pages/870/Industrialization-Family.html.

Jefferson, Thomas. "From Thomas Jefferson to John Blair, 13 August 1787." https://founders.archives.gov/documents/Jefferson/01-12-02-0031.

———. "From Thomas Jefferson to John Jay, 23 August 1785." http://founders.archives.gov/documents/Jefferson/01-08-02-0333.

———. "Thomas Jefferson to James Madison." http://press-pubs.uchicago.edu/founders/documents/v1ch15s32.html.

———. "From Thomas Jefferson to Thomas Cooper, 29 November 1802." http://founders.archives.gov/documents/Jefferson/01-39-02-0070.

Jerman, Jenna, et al. "Characteristics of U.S. Abortion Patients in 2014 and Changes Since 2008." https://www.guttmacher.org/report/characteristics-us-abortion-patients-2014.

Johnson, Kenneth. *Demographic Trends in Rural and Small Town America*. Durham, NH: University of New Hampshire, Carsey Institute, 2006. https://scholars.unh.edu/cgi/viewcontent.cgi?article=1004&context=carsey.

Judd, Richard W. *Common Lands, Common People: The Origins of Conservation in Northern New England*. Cambridge: Harvard University Press, 1997.

Kerridge, Richard. "Environmentalism and Ecocriticism." *Literary Theory and Criticism: An Oxford Guide*, edited by Patricia Waugh, 530–44. Oxford: Oxford University Press, 2006.

Kimball, Roger. "Some Perils of Sexual Liberation." https://www.newcriterion.com/blogs/dispatch/some-perils-of-sexual-liberation.

Kirk, Marshall, and Hunter Madsen. "The Overhauling of Straight America." http://library.gayhomeland.org/0018/EN/EN_Overhauling_Straight.htm.

Kurtzweil, Ray. *The Age of Spiritual Machines: When Computers Exceed Human Intelligence*. New York: Viking, 1999.

Lattin, Don. "Dali Lama Speaks on Gay Sex / He Says It's Wrong for Buddhists but Not for Society." *San Francisco Chronicle*, June 11, 1997. http://www.sfgate.com/news/article/Dalai-Lama-Speaks-on-Gay-Sex-He-says-it-s-wrong-2836591.php.

"Leading Causes of Death in Females (current listing)." https://www.cdc.gov/women/lcod/2014/all-females/index.htm.

Leopold, Aldo. "The State of the Profession." In *The River of the Mother of God*, edited by Susan L. Flader and J. Baird Callicott, 276–80. Madison: University of Wisconsin Press, 1991.

———. "Threatened Species." In *The River of the Mother of God*, edited by Susan L. Flader and J. Baird Callicott, 230–34. Madison: University of Wisconsin Press, 1991.

"LGBT." https://en.wikipedia.org/wiki/LGBT.

Lott, Melissa C. "10 Calories In, 1 Calorie Out—The Energy We Spend on Food." *Scientific American*, August 11, 2011. https://blogs.scientificamerican.com/plugged-in/10-calories-in-1-calorie-out-the-energy-we-spend-on-food/.

Lytle, Andrew Nelson. "The Hind Tit." In *I'll Take My Stand: The South and the Agrarian Tradition*, by John Crowe Ransom et al., 201–45. Baton Rouge: Louisiana State University Press, 1958.

Macon & Wester Railroad Co. v. Lester. 30 Ga. 911 (1860).

Bibliography

May, Meredith. "S.F.'s Best Friend: Where Pooches Outnumber Kids, Impassioned, Doting Owners and Hounds Dressed to the Canines Treat All Days Like Dog Days." *SFGate*, June 17, 2007. http://www.sfgate.com/news/article/S-F-S-BEST-FRIEND-Where-pooches-outnumber-2555688.php.

McLaughlin, Dan. "Can Gays and Christians Coexist In America? Part 1: To Make Christians do What the Gay Lobby Demands Would Eradicate Their Religion Entirely." *The Federalist*, June 8, 2015. http://thefederalist.com/2015/06/08/can-gays-and-christians-coexist-in-america-part-1/.

———. "Can Gays and Christians Coexist In America? Part III: To Make Christians do What the Gay Lobby Demands Would Eradicate Their Religion Entirely." *The Federalist*, June 10, 2015. http://thefederalist.com/2015/06/10/can-gays-and-christians-coexist-in-america-part-iii/.

Mendelsohn, Daniel. "We're Here, We're Queer, Let's Get Coffee: If You Look Straight, Act Straight, and Think Straight, Why Bother to be Gay? Notes on the Mainstreaming of a Once-Edgy Subculture." *New York Magazine*, September 30, 1996.

Migeon, Gerard. "Can the Birth Control Pill Cause Birth Defects?" *Natural Womanhood*, January 16, 2016. https://naturalwomanhood.org/can-the-birth-control-pill-cause-birth-defects/.

Mill, John Stuart. "On Liberty." http://www.gutenberg.org/ebooks/34901?msg=welcome_stranger.

Miller v. Texas, 153 U.S. 535 (1894). https://supreme.justia.com/cases/federal/us/153/535/case.html.

Mondimore, Mark. *A Natural History of Homosexuality*. Baltimore: Johns Hopkins University Press, 1996.

Moravec, Hans. *Mind Children: The Future of Robots and Human Intelligence*. Cambridge: Harvard University Press, 1998.

Mueller, Walt. "What You Need to Know About TV Violence." https://cpyu.org/resource/what-you-need-to-know-about-tv-violence/.

Our Bodies, Ourselves for the New Century. New York: Touchstone, 1998.

"Our History." https://www.plannedparenthood.org/about-us/who-we-are/our-history.

Podhoretz, Norman. "How the Gay-Rights Movement Won." *Commentary Magazine*, November 1, 1996. https://www.commentarymagazine.com/articles/how-the-gay-rights-movement-won/.

"Population & Migration: Overview." https://www.ers.usda.gov/topics/rural-economy-population/population-migration/.

Ravitz, Jessica. "The Surprising History of Abortion in the United States." CNN, June 27, 2016. http://www.cnn.com/2016/06/23/health/abortion-history-in-united-states/index.html.

Reynolds v. the U.S. 98 U.S. 145 (1878). http://caselaw.findlaw.com/us-supreme-court/98/145.html.

Roosevelt, Theodore. "John Muir: An Appreciation." *The Outlook: An Illustrated Weekly Journal of Current Life*, 109 (January 16, 1915) 27–28.

———. "Seventh Annual Message, December 3, 1907." http://www.presidency.ucsb.edu/ws/index.php?pid=29548.

Rowan, Chris. "The Impact of Technology on the Developing Child." *Huffington Post*, May 29, 2013. http://www.huffingtonpost.com/cris-rowan/technology-children-negative-impact_b_3343245.html.

Sanger, Margaret. *The Pivot of Civilization*. Reprint, Elmsford, NY: 1969.

Bibliography

Shilts, Randy. *And the Band Played On: Politics, People, and the AIDS Epidemic.* Reprint, New York: St. Martin's Griffin, 2007.

Smith, Nicole. "The Impacts of the Industrial Revolution on Families in New England and America." http://www.articlemyriad.com/impacts-industrial-revolution-families-new-england/.

Soros, George. "The Capitalist Threat." *The Atlantic Monthly* 279.2 (1997) 45–58.

Stern, Karl. *The Flight from Woman.* St. Paul: Paragon, 1965.

Stoll, Stephen. *Larding the Lean Earth: Soil and Society in Nineteenth-Century America.* New York: Hill and Wang, 2002.

Stuntz, William J. "When Rights are Wrong." *First Things*, April 1, 1996. https://www.firstthings.com/article/1996/04/001-when-rights-are-wrong.

"Theodore Roosevelt." http://vault.sierraclub.org/john_muir_exhibit/people/roosevelt.aspx.

"Theodore Roosevelt and Conservation." https://www.nps.gov/thro/learn/historyculture/theodore-roosevelt-and-conservation.htm.

Tingle, Rachel. "The Ideology and Politics of the Gay Movement." http://trushare.com/29OCT97/imptingl.txt.

United States Census Bureau. "Measuring America." https://www.census.gov/library/visualizations/2016/comm/acs-rural-urban.html.

"Unmarried Childbearing." https://www.cdc.gov/nchs/fastats/unmarried-childbearing.htm.

"Violence in the Media and Entertainment (Position Paper)." https://www.aafp.org/about/policies/all/violence-media.html.

Warren, Robert Penn. "The Briar Patch." In *I'll Take My Stand: The South and the Agrarian Tradition*, by John Crowe Ransom et al., 246–64. Baton Rouge: Louisiana State University Press, 1958.

"What is Cancer?" http://www.web-books.com/eLibrary/Medicine/Cancer/01MB9.html.

"Who We Are." https://www.plannedparenthood.org/about-us/who-we-are.

"Why Does the Individual Need Freedom?" http://capitalism.org/freedom/why-does-the-individual-need-freedom/.

Xue, Katherine. "Is There an App for That?" *Harvard Magazine*, November–December 2013. http://harvardmagazine.com/2013/11/is-there-an-app-for-that.

Young, Stark. "Not in Memoriam, But in Defense." In *I'll Take My Stand: The South and the Agrarian Tradition*, by John Crowe Ransom et al., 328–60. Baton Rouge: Louisiana State University Press, 1958.

Zimmer, Carl. "Unraveling the Mystery of the Bizarre Deformed Frogs." https://e360.yale.edu/features/unraveling_the_mystery_of_the_bizarre_deformed_frogs.

"Zoophiles March on Berlin to Demand Equal Rights." https://www.webpronews.com/zoophiles-march-on-berlin-to-demand-equal-rights/.

www.ingramcontent.com/pod-product-compliance
Lightning Source LLC
Chambersburg PA
CBHW051937160426
43198CB00013B/2195